D1276349

PLATONISM

PLATONISM

BY

PAUL ELMER MORE

THIRD EDITION

B
395
.M8
1969

AMS PRESS
NEW YORK

Reprinted from the third edition of 1931, Princeton
First AMS EDITION published 1969
Manufactured in the United States of America

Library of Congress Catalogue Card Number: 77-98631

AMS PRESS, INC.
New York, N.Y. 10003

HC 11-21

Wherefore we must discriminate between two kinds of cause, the one of necessity, the other divine; and the divine cause we must seek in all things, to the end that we may possess a happy life so far as our nature permits; and the necessary cause for the sake of the divine, reflecting that otherwise we cannot apprehend by themselves those truths which are the object of our serious study, nor grasp them or in any other way partake of them.—Timaeus 68E.

From this source we have derived philosophy, than which no greater good ever was or will be given by the gods to mortal man.—Ibid. 47A.

PREFACE TO THIRD EDITION

THE substance of the following chapters was prepared for the Vanuxem lectures given at Princeton in the autumn of 1917. At that time, as stated in the preface to the first edition of *Platonism,* I had already formed the project of a series of volumes on the Greek Tradition, the writing of which was to occupy the expected years of leisure newly won from journalism, and the purpose of which, again as stated in the first preface, was to deal with the origins and early environment of Christianity and with more modern revivals of the Platonic philosophy. But the plan was then vaguely conceived, and in particular the scope of the material to be included was left to be determined as the work progressed and as time permitted. To this fact must be attributed certain changes in programme as announced in successive advertisements. As now completed the work, or, more precisely I might say, the core of the work, consists of four volumes, beginning with *The Religion of Plato,* passing to a study of what may be regarded as a divagation from the true line of Greek thought in the various *Hellenistic Philosophies,* and from that to the origin of the Christian faith in the New Testament and its consummation in the blending of the Greek and Hebrew Traditions to form the theology of the Incarnate Word. To these are added two complementary volumes: the present more general manual of *Platonism* as an introduction, and *The Catholic Faith* as a supplement. A survey of the Aristotelian philosophy is in active preparation, and other complementary volumes are planned but may or may not be achieved.

More important than the change of programme affecting the scope of the material included is a certain shift of emphasis in the treatment of the material, which I know has troubled some readers as an inconsistency, and about which it may be in place here to say a word. I would not deny that the attitude towards religion is not quite the same in the first edition of this volume and in the later volumes on Christianity and the Catholic faith. And though in revising this introductory work for a second edition it would have been easy to eliminate or smooth over the apparent inconsistencies, I thought it less confusing and more honest to leave them to speak for themselves. And furthermore, as was said in the preface to that revision, something might be learnt from a change which I should like to esteem a growth in insight on the part of the writer, as it unquestionably was the result of enlarged knowledge.

The point of view from which these studies of the Greek Tradition were begun may best be stated by quoting from the preface to the first edition of *Platonism*:

"Only through the centralizing force of religious faith or through its equivalent in philosophy can the intellectual life regain its meaning and authority for earnest men. Yet, for the present at least, the dogmas of religion have lost their hold, while the current philosophy of the schools has become in large measure a quibbling of specialists on technical points of minor importance, or, where serious, too commonly has surrendered to that flattery of the instinctive elements of human nature which is the very negation of mental and moral discipline.

"It is in such a belief and such a hope, whether right or wrong, that I have turned back to the truth, still potent and fresh and salutary, which Plato expounded in the troubled and doubting days of Greece—the truth which is in religion but is not bounded by religious dogma, and which needs no confirmation by miracle or inspired tradition. The first task before me was to see this philosophy in its naked outlines, stripped of its confusing accessories, and cleared of the misunderstandings which, starting among the barbarians of Alexandria, have made of Platonism too often a support instead of a corrective of the disintegrating forces of society. This I have attempted to do, with imperfect success no doubt, in the present volume."

The truth which is in religion but is not bounded by religious dogma,—it is this that I sought to clarify and expound in the Vanuxem lectures, and it is to this that I looked for a guiding thread through the projected study of Christian origins. And from that point of view there has been no retreat. It seemed to me then that in the Platonic doctrine of Ideas such a truth was once given to the world, and that without a conviction of spiritual and moral values as dynamic realities to which all our thinking and all our acting are in some way held responsible, to which even the Power behind the world, whether it be named the Demiurge of Plato or the Jehovah of Christian theology, must submit for the norm of creative energy, —it still seems to me that deprived of this conviction our talk about philosophy is empty chatter and our religion a progress to the abysmal void of pantheism or absolute transcendentalism. It is the same truth, somewhat differently formulated, that in the wisdom of the East appears as the stupendous belief in Karma. It is the truth, I am sure, by which the man in the street, so long as his mind has not been perverted by confused echoes from the schools, guides his faltering footsteps. It springs from the deepest and most constant experience of life, deeper and more constant than the syllogistic conclusions of reason, and without it our discussions are vain and our hopes of mutual understanding foredoomed. As St. Augustine says: *Si non sit intus qui doceat inanis fit strepitus noster.*

But is it a fact that this truth *needs no confirmation by miracle or inspired tradition*? Fresh and salutary the Platonic doctrine of Ideas still is, as it has ever been, but of its potency, unsupported by outer signs, I began to be not so sure. Longer reflection on the events of history and on the needs of human nature raised the persistent question whether just such a confirmation was not required if Platonism was to be converted from a mental luxury for the few to a faith which could stir the sluggish heart of the world, to a power indeed which could meet the spiritual demands of the individual soul. So it happened that I came in the course of my studies to see in the central dogma of Christianity as it were a realization in fact of the dualism which Plato had divined as a theorem of philosophy, and the foreordained consummation of the Greek Tradition. What had allured the mind as a beautiful myth assumed gradually the awful dignity of revelation. In this sense it may be affirmed that *Christ the Word* and *The Catholic Faith* are not inconsistent with this introductory volume, though the point of view has in a manner changed.

It only remains to be said that the text of this third edition is identical with that of the second.

P. E. M.

25 May, 1931.

CONTENTS

PLATONISM

CHAPTER I

THE THREE SOCRATIC THESES

NO other person of antiquity, scarcely any of the modern world, has been portrayed so vividly as the master whom Plato made the responsible mouthpiece of his speculations. We seem to descry the man Socrates in the very flesh; we can almost hear his voice, as he talked with friends and strangers in the agora and other meeting-places of Athens. But when we come to consider him as a philosopher in his own right, and to determine precisely what he taught, the way is not so plain. Of the two main witnesses on whom we must rely for our knowledge of his teaching, the one, our gossiping Xenophon, understood him too little, whereas the other understood him, in a manner, too well, developing his instruction into so rich and voluminous a body of thought that Socrates might have exclaimed with some apparent reason, as indeed he is said actually to have done on hearing one of the simpler of Plato's Dialogues: "By Heracles, what lies the young man has told about me!" Our conception of the Socratic philosophy is thus, like the Eros of the wonderful woman of Mantinea, the child of Penury and Abundance—an Abundance, we might add, "drunken with the drink of the gods."

Yet withal the leading theses of Socrates are in themselves, and taken separately, clear enough—or ought to be so to anyone who approaches the subject with open mind—and the real difficulty begins only when we undertake to combine them into a coherent system, and to weigh their remoter consequences. These leading doctrines, if we may give such a name to the impulses that carried him towards philosophy, were three: an intellectual scepticism, a spiritual affirmation, and a tenacious belief in the identity of virtue and knowledge.

Of the sceptical, questioning disposition of Socrates we have ample testimony. This was the trait, particularly as it touched the common tradition in matters of government and morals, that most impressed those of his contemporaries who did not belong to the inner circle of disciples. And probably the irony of Socrates, his real or feigned ignorance used as a dissolvent of the assumed knowledge of others, is the characteristic first suggested today by the mention of his name. He himself, when obliged to defend his life before the tribunal of his fellow citizens, manfully admitted this scepticism, and even claimed for it a divine sanction. One of his friends, so he declared, had gone to Delphi to inquire of the oracle whether there was any one wiser than Socrates, and had been told that there was none wiser. Whereupon Socrates, amazed and incredulous, had put himself to the task of testing this strange saying. His method of inquiry (which we may suppose he had employed from the beginning of his public career, though with less deliberate purpose before the intervention of the oracle) was to select a man eminent for wisdom, and to cross-question him about his knowledge; and this he did repeatedly, and always with the same result. "It would soon become apparent," he says, "that to many people, and most of all to himself, the man seemed to be wise, whereas in truth he was not so at all. Thereupon I would try to show him how he was wise in opinion only and not in reality; but I merely made myself a nuisance to him and to many of those about him. So I used to go away reflecting that at least I was wiser than this man. Neither of us, I would say to myself, knows anything much worth while, but he in his ignorance thinks he knows, whereas I neither know nor think I know."[1]

But if the existence, even the predominance, of the doubting mood in Socrates cannot be overlooked, the quality of this scepticism needs none the less to be sharply distinguished from what commonly passes under the name. The matter stands thus. Absolute suspension of judgement, however a man may profess it in words or strive to attain it in practice, is an impossibility. You may deny the power of human reason to explain the cause and ultimate nature of things; but the moment you do this, you will find yourself, if you examine your mind honestly, putting credence in some faculty either above the reason or below the reason. Some relation to appearances you must assume, some motive of action you are bound to obey, some affirmation you are forced to make;[2]

[1] I hold for many reasons that the biographical parts of the *Apology, Crito,* and *Phaedo* present a faithful picture of the man Socrates, and in the main give a true account of his last days, however the glamour of Plato's rhetoric may lie over the whole. It is easier to believe in the power of Nature to create such a character than in the ability of an author to imagine it. Furthermore, though Xenophon probably had little intercourse with Socrates and certainly was no philosopher, yet he gives the same report of Socrates' ordinary ways of life, and one can find in the *Memorabilia* clear traces of the Socratic theses.

[2] This fact is virtually acknowledged by the clever exponent of ancient scepticism, Sextus Empiricus. See his *Hypotyposes* i, 17, *et passim.* As for modern agnostics, so-called, they too reserve their scepticism for the "unknowable" things of the spirit, and are thorough-going dogmatists in their own field of interest.

the only choice is to which of the alternative solicitations you will say yes, and to which you will say no. Thus, when a man calls himself a sceptic, it commonly means that he subscribes to some form of materialistic dogma, and practically believes that pleasures and pains of the body, however he may refine and intellectualize their quality, are the one certain fact of experience. As the followers of Aristippus used to say: "Only our sensations are comprehensible." This creed may be adopted from mere indolence of mind, or in the combative manner of the schools—but with results curiously alike. According to his first disciple, Pyrrho, the father of professional scepticism, reduced the problems of philosophy to these three: "What is the nature of things? How should we be disposed towards them? What is the consequence to us of this determination?" The answer was that we know nothing of the great forces playing about us, and that he is wise who, freeing his soul of troublesome fears or questions, does not look beyond the pleasure within his reach.[3] There is a pretty parable that tells how Pyrrho enforced this doctrine. Being once at sea and caught in a storm, he rebuked the terror of the passengers by pointing to a little pig that kept on feeding through all the commotion—such, he said, ought to be the

Phaedo 83B

[3] See Eusebius, *Praeparatio Evangelica* xiv, 18, 2.

tranquillity of the wise man. There is an affirmation in this—deck and disguise it as you will—the affirmation of the sty: *pinguem et nitidum vises Epicuri de grege porcum.* Such a man may call himself a philosophical sceptic by reason of his anti-rationalism, but his philosophy comes from a plane below the reason, and is hard to distinguish from the indolent self-assurance that is content to do without thinking at all.

If we take the word "sceptic" in its truer sense, as describing one who takes nothing on trust but examines the facts of experience to their last conclusion, the Epicurean or Pyrrhonist has no right to the name, since he still labours under the delusion of supposing he knows what he does not know, and has yet to learn that pleasure and pain have no final value in themselves, but must be estimated by their relation to values of quite another order. Manifestly, at least, the scepticism of Socrates was no Pyrrhonic drifting with the current of opinion; it meant to him rather an unwearied questioning of the solicitations of both the reason and the senses, and a continuous exercise of the will, being of all states of mind the rarest and the most difficult for a man in this world to maintain. Doubt was thus to Socrates the beginning both of philosophy and of morality—of philosophy, since only those are prompted to philosophize truly who are ignorant and, at the same time, aware of their ignorance; of morality, since only those will feel the compelling of a higher impulse who have seen through the illusory curtain of the senses. When Socrates came to explain to the court why he had not hesitated in a course of action which was sure to bring him into peril of losing what most men prize, including life itself, he replied boldly that he had followed the behest of the God for the reason that of those so-called perils we have no real knowledge—not even of the greatest of them. "For the fear of death," he said, "is just another form of appearing wise when we are foolish, and of seeming to know what we know not. No mortal knoweth of death whether it be not the greatest of all good things to man, yet do men fear it as if they knew it to be the greatest of evils. And is not this that most culpable ignorance which pretends to know what it knows not?" This sounds like the parable of Pyrrho and his pig; but note the difference in the consequences drawn. Socrates was not contradicting himself, but was basing his conduct on a profounder form of scepticism than Pyrrho's, when, in one and the same discourse, he avowed that his only wisdom was to know his own ignorance, yet declared himself ready to face death with this downright affirmation: "To do wrong and to disobey our superior,

Lysis 218A

Apology 29A

whether human or divine, this I do know to be an evil and shameful thing." He had an invincible assurance of this spiritual fact for the very reason that his scepticism went deep enough to include those current judgements and those immediate values of sensation which to a Pyrrho were the only certain guides through the perplexities of life.

There is, then, no inconsistency in the union of intellectual scepticism and spiritual affirmation; rather, scepticism is the negative aspect of the same intuitive truth of which spiritual affirmation is the positive aspect. It would even be a grave error—the gravest of all errors in its possible consequences—to reckon the sceptical attitude, because it is purely negative, as less essential to the Socratic life than its positive counterpart. It is, if anything, more essential; for its authority extends in a way beyond reason and the senses to the highest citadel of the soul. Our one safeguard against a host of ruinous deceptions that speak in the name of the spirit is the obstinate interrogation of every affirmation of every sort, and the holding of each presumptive truth to give proof of itself in experience. In later years these two aspects of Socratic doctrine were developed independently into separate schools, the sceptic, of which we have spoken, and the Neoplatonic. If

Socrates had been alive, and had been forced to choose between the books of a Sextus Empiricus, let us say, who in the name of scepticism rejected all authority of reason and the higher intuition, and the books of a Proclus, who accepted almost without discrimination any words uttered in the name of the spirit, he would have ranged himself, I am sure, with Sextus, and would have expended his powers of irony upon the religious jargon of the self-styled Platonist. He would have preferred the half-truth of the one to the sham-truth of the other; and Plato would have made the same choice.

But if it is easy to see how true scepticism and spiritual intuition may go hand in hand, the case is different when to these two theses we add the third. It was one of Socrates' favorite maxims that no man errs, or sins, willingly, but only through ignorance—a saying hard to reconcile with the actual conduct of the world, hard to reconcile with the other aspects of the Socratic doctrine. On its face this maxim implies an equation of virtue and knowledge, and by knowledge the evidence obliges us to believe that Socrates meant, not indeed a Pyrrhonic acquiescence in the solicitations of the present, but that larger calculation of life in the terms of pleasure and pain which from his day to this has been the mark of the rationalizing utilitarian. As we know better, he would say, the near and remote consequences of our acts in those terms, we are enabled to conduct ourselves more prudently; and this prudence is virtue. How, one asks in some bewilderment, can a teacher maintain such a thesis as this, yet as a sceptic reject the authority of the senses, and as a mystic avow that his morality depends on a super-rational intuition? How can the same man be a rationalizing utilitarian and a sceptical mystic?

However perplexing such a union of contraries may appear to us, we have nothing to do but to accept the paradox as it stands. Above all we must not emphasize the rationalistic thesis so as to suppress the other two. In that way we should fall into the totally inadequate conception of Socrates made current today by the *Greek Thinkers* of Theodor Gomperz. According to that brilliant and much-quoted history, the Platonic Socrates, with his religious and fundamentally sceptical traits, is to be rejected for a mere questioner of popular tradition and promoter of the rationalistic "Enlightenment." The story in the *Apology* of his self-dedication to the service of the God is pure moonshine; Socrates had one simple aim, to set forth the unity of virtue and knowledge, and to that end there was no need of exhortation or animating appeal, no room for any positive ethical teaching based on an authority higher than reason. Now the Socrates of this school of interpreters is an impossibility—a creature manufactured in a Teutonic *phrontistêrion,* and not the living man of Athens from whom the deepest inspiration of philosophy has flowed even to this day. Gomperz himself offers a corrective to his portrait by quoting as the motto for his volume this sentence from Clement of Alexandria: "Wherefore also Cleanthes in his second book Concerning Pleasure says that Socrates always identified the just man and the happy man, and *cursed* him who first distinguished between the just and the profitable *as one who had done an impious thing.*" There is decidedly something of the exhorter and preacher of virtue in the words italicized, though we need not, for all that, picture Socrates quite as a Lutheran parson. If Clement is right, and Plato was not a mere mystificator, and if human nature has any place in the study of philosophy, then Gomperz is wrong. We may be certain that beneath the irony of Socrates, deeper than his questioning of popular phrases and his search for precision of definition, lay a power of very positive teaching and a direct appeal to the conscience, in his own way and at his own time, which smote the heart even of such a worldling as Alcibiades to the quick, and shall never cease to vibrate in the hearts of living men. Plutarch was in the right tradition when, remembering the confession of Alcibiades, he said that "outwardly Socrates to those who met him appeared rude and uncouth and overbearing, but within was full of earnestness and of matters that moved his hearers to tears and wrung their hearts."[4]

On the other hand we must be on our guard against the contrary extreme of those scholars who, in their laudable desire to reinstate Socrates as a religious teacher and seer, go so far as to make a harsh division between the rationalistic and the mystical elements in the Platonic Dialogues, and then relegate all the former to Plato himself and derive all the latter from Socrates. Professor Burnet[5] would even have us believe that in the earlier Dialogues, down to and including *The Republic,* Plato was merely reproducing as a dramatic artist the mystic and idealistic Pythagoreanism of his master, whereas in the later Dialogues he breaks away from this and gives expression to his own scientific and anti-Socratic rationalism. Now, with all due deference to the great learning of Professor Burnet, one must say that such a theory has no warrant in history or in common sense. To assert that a man could write

[4] *Cato* vii.
[5] *Greek Philosophy,* Part I, pp. 178, 179ff.

The Republic without a definite philosophy of his own is to run pretty close to a pedantic absurdity; and it is not much better to maintain that there was no rationalism in the teaching of Socrates than that there was no mysticism in the teaching of Plato.

The efforts of various scholars to escape the Socratic Paradox by representing him on the one hand as a pure rationalist or on the other hand as a pure mystic are equally untenable. So far as we can judge from the records, Socrates never attempted to find an interpretation of the word "knowledge" which should reconcile his third thesis with the other two, nor did he even, we may suppose, see quite so logical a synthesis of his intellectual scepticism and higher intuition as we have felt justified in deriving from the language of the *Apology*. For the most part he was content, it should appear, to enunciate his three principles as independent truths, and to enforce now one and now another of them as occasion prompted, leaving to his disciples, the creators of the so-called Socratic schools, the labour of constructing from them what properly may be regarded as a philosophic system. Endless inconsistencies and controversies were to arise among his successors from the varying emphasis placed by them on the different aspects of his creed. To

Plato alone it was given to combine the three theses without sacrificing one for the other, and so to develop a philosophy that transcended the master's actual teaching while in no fundamental matter betraying it. So successfully did he accomplish this great task that to the world at large Socrates has come to stand for little more than a mouthpiece of the Platonic speculations. Nevertheless we shall be doing a grave injustice if, caught by the spell of Plato's richer and subtler genius, we forget that the imposing enunciation of his three doctrines by Plato's teacher was the determining event in the moral and religious life of the Western world; for the supreme need of a man's soul is not that he should acquire a splendid system of philosophy, but that he should hold as an inexpugnable possession that spirit of scepticism and insight and that assurance of the identity of virtue and knowledge for which Socrates lived and died.[6]

Yet however important, even revolutionary, the work of Socrates may appear, we must remember that he was only one teacher among many; nor can we rightly understand the Pla-

[6] The Christian philosophy of Pascal is founded on three similar principles: "Il faut avoir ces trois qualités, pyrrhonien, géomètre, Chrétien soumis; et elles s'accordent, et se tempèrent, en doutant où il faut, en assurant où il faut, et en se soumettant où il faut.—*Pensée* 268, Brunschvicg.

tonic philosophy without taking into account the strong currents of thought, sympathetic and antipathetic, amid which it took its origin. The age of Socrates was notable for an intellectual curiosity and a moral fermentation for which there is perhaps only one parallel in history, and that parallel takes us out of Europe to Asia. There, in the country of the Ganges, at a somewhat earlier date, the old formalities of religion had ceased to satisfy the devout Hindu worshipper, and he could no longer accept the traditional precepts of morality until he had justified them at the bar of his own conscience. Everywhere men were asking themselves and one another about the underlying truth of things, and a rumour went abroad that certain lonely explorers had discovered a treasure of knowledge which they held as a secret possession. And so the books of the period were filled with stories, some of them quaint and obscure, others very beautiful, of eager inquirers who went out into the wilderness, where the sages had their solitary abodes, to question and listen, and to learn, if they were deemed worthy, the new meaning of the old words of religion and morality.

Something like that, though the methods of teaching and the final results were different, was going on in Greece during the lifetime of Socrates. The supposed possessors of the secret were not eremites hiding in the forest depths, but teachers who called themselves sophists and went about from city to city imparting instruction for a price; and the inquirers who flocked to their lectures were not, for the most part, religious enthusiasts, but young men of family who were looking for the readiest path to honour and power in civic life. Yet, withal, the mental and moral ferments were much the same as in India, and in both lands the deepest problems of law and faith did not pass through the ordeal untouched.

Not the least extraordinary of Plato's literary gifts is his skill in reproducing in a colder age the ardour which surrounded his childhood and youth. In the opening of such a Dialogue as the *Protagoras,* for instance, there is a note of excitement, of expectation, which carries the reader back to a society stirred by a veritable renaissance of wonder. Even the more conservative citizens were moved, some to hostility, some to friendly curiosity. So, in the *Theages,* we have a charmingly realistic picture of an elderly man, of position and property, coming into Athens from the country to consult Socrates about the education of his son; for the boy has heard rumours of the marvellous cunning of these professors who are flocking to the city from the ends of the world, and is determined to place himself as a pupil under one of them. The father, as befits a solid man of the soil, is bewildered and anxious; he doesn't mind spending the necessary money, but he has his suspicion of these innovations and he fears they are as likely to corrupt as to inform. Whereupon Socrates turns to the young man, and quizzes him to bring out just what he thinks this new wisdom is and what it will do for him.

Now to many scholars of our age Socrates was not much different from any other of these votaries of new-fangled ideas; and, superficially, there is some basis for this fatal confusion. But the moment we apply to these wandering teachers the test of the three Socratic theses we see that in their attitude towards the central truth of philosophy they stood at the opposite pole from Socrates; we see, too, how deeply the intellectual and moral destiny of Greece was involved in this difference.

Some of the sophists may have been inclined to dogmatic rationalism, and could therefore scarcely be called sceptics in any sense of the word. But for the most part they were questioners and innovators by profession, in harmony with the common unrest of the times. Their general position is fairly expressed in the famous maxim of Protagoras, that "Man is the measure of all things." Such a principle might seem on its face—as it has seemed to certain modern critics—to be

Theaetetus 152A

in accord with Socrates' habit of putting the received laws of conduct to the test of human experience; and this indeed would be the case, were it not for the utterly diverse meanings that may be attached to the word "man." Now Protagoras had in mind to say that right and wrong are matters of human opinion, being actually to each man as his good pleasure thinks them to be. More than that, they not only vary in their nature with the opinions of different men, but depend on the changing moods of each individual man, so that what is right and just for me at this moment may be at another moment the very reverse of right and just. In other words, by "man" Protagoras meant the impression of the senses and the dictates of temperament, and virtually denied the existence of that unchanging law on which Socrates based his conduct when he declared himself ignorant of all things save of this one fact, that it is better for a man to be just than to be unjust, and better, if needs be, to suffer wrong than to do wrong.

The issue between the two ways of life is brought out more sharply by adding to the Protagorean maxim already quoted his other famous saying, that of the gods we have no knowledge whether they are or are not, and by contrasting with these statements the terse epigram of Plato, that, if we

Theaetetus 162D

cared for our happiness, "Not any man, as some say, but God would be the measure of all things." Plato, when he wrote these words in his old age, was thinking of the transcendent Creator and Lord of Providence; but even so he had not forgotten his earlier belief in that element of the human soul itself which was akin to the deity in form and power. He too, in his way, made man the measure of all things; but by man he had learnt from his master to think first, not of the opinions that separate one man from another and a man today from himself of yesterday, but of the divine principle that is the same in all men and forms therefore the only true bond of friendship and society. It was just this principle of the innate divine that Protagoras denied—certainly at least Plato so understood him—when he made man the measure of truth and avowed that of the gods there was no way of knowing whether they were or were not. And, whatever apparent exceptions there may have been here and there, Protagoras was in this representative of the whole body of the sophists. By omitting the Socratic affirmation from their scheme of life they turned their philosophy, so far as they had any, in the direction of that Pyrrhonic scepticism which is the very contrary of the Socratic.

Laws 716c

Republic 501B

The same essential difference between Socrates

and the sophists comes out when we pass from scepticism and spiritual affirmation to the third thesis. So far as it is possible to group together men who formed no cohesive party, but professed each after his own desire, the sophists were at least in agreement among themselves in the belief that virtue and knowledge are somehow identical; in fact it was their avowed mission to impart the knowledge requisite for virtue, as the thing virtue was commonly understood. And they had a useful function to perform. Their instruction was partly of a purely objective sort, and as such valuable in itself. As for their rhetoric, Socrates did not hesitate to admit that he had acquired some of his perfectly legitimate skill in the use of words from Prodicus and other such teachers. And so, in the absence of schools beyond the most elementary sort, the sophists must enjoy the credit of sharing in the advancement of practical education. Even here, indeed, we begin to see the divergence between their method and that of Socrates, for Socrates was too genuinely sceptical, of himself as well as of others, to go about like an ambulatory university lecturing for a fee on any province of science or art then known to mankind. But that is a minor matter. The serious divergence was in their purpose. If there be any truth in Plato's account of the debates between Socrates and such masters of the craft as Gorgias and Protagoras, it is clear that the sophists directed their instruction chiefly to the acquisition of skill in manipulating individual men and popular assemblies. I do not mean to say, following an ancient accusation, that the sophists set out deliberately to instruct men in the art of making the better cause appear the worse, in the sense that they had any vicious or anti-social end in view; but rather that they had in view no end at all, except the end of success. Their concern was very much with practical cleverness and very little with moral consequences, very much with current opinion and very little with truth for its own sake; hence the supreme place of rhetoric in their curriculum, as the art of persuasion. They would have accepted as readily as Socrates the identification of virtue and knowledge; but they identified the two by making them both a means, without stopping to ask themselves or others the means to *what*. In the quest of that *what* Socrates was to pass his life; and if he was still searching and had not reached the goal of the great quest when death put an end to all his asking, it was because he had not clearly discovered the relation of the knowledge that determines virtue to the knowledge that belongs to scepticism and spiritual affirmation.

Such is the contrast between Socrates and the sophists the moment we apply to them the test of the three theses. To ignore this radical difference in favour of the surface resemblances, as has been somewhat the practice since Grote's powerful rehabilitation of the sophists, is to overlook the whole significance of the Socratic teaching, and it is to miss terribly the tragic lesson of history. This was no paltry feud over scholastic terms, but the battle of one man who saw the truth and knew the consequences of error against a host of men who looked upon the truth with the eyes of a Pontius Pilate; rather, it was the battle of one man for the deeper common sense of mankind against the sophistries of a people who had lost their anchorage and were drifting they knew not whither.

The Greeks are distinguished from other great peoples by their lack of any really sacred books or of a definite revelation; and to this freedom of their imagination we owe a religion which of all religions is the most purely human and the best adapted to the service of art and poetry. It is almost as full of meaning today, for those who understand it, as it was to the contemporaries of Socrates. But this freedom was a peril also, as all liberty is perilous. In an age of doubt and egoistic revolt from tradition such a religion, unless its deeper meaning meets with some authentication in the individual consciousness, is peculiarly liable to lose its moral hold and to become a plaything for the fancy of its votaries. This is the easy way; it was the direction in which the educated classes of Greece were naturally turning, and the Protagorean scepticism, with its flattering plausibility, was ready at hand to cloak moral indolence in the garb of philosophy.

The Greeks, again, as we see them typified from the beginning in Odysseus, were inclined to cleverness and versatility more than to plain truth, and prone to lay weight on the value of worldly wisdom somewhat at the expense of instinctive rectitude. They were always a little too quick to applaud knowledge for its own sake and to measure virtue by the standard of success. And this disposition was fostered by the sophists at a critical moment of history. Plato laid his finger on one of the spots where the decay of national character first discovered itself, when he declared that for the rhetorician, trained to plead before the courts, there was no need to bother over the exact nature of justice and goodness, since no juror would take heed of such subtleties, but would be guided in his vote by the force of persuasion based on probability. Any one conversant with the literature of the Greek people knows how large a place

Phaedrus 272D

the word "probable" occupies in their whole manner of thinking, and how cunningly the sophistical game played with the national foible.

What came in the end of this itching cleverness and this adroit flattery can be read in the Roman estimate of Greece in her degeneracy:

> *Augur schoenobates medicus magus, omnia novit*
> *Graeculus esuriens; in caelum miseris, ibit.*[7]

Or, if it seems unfair to accept the petulant satire of Juvenal as historical evidence, some credit at least must be allowed to Cicero's comparison of Greek and Roman witnesses under oath. "He had," he says, in his oration ***Pro Flacco,*** "always been particularly addicted to that nation and their studies, and knew many modest and worthy men among them. But as to the sanctity of an oath, they had no notion of it; all their concern in giving evidence was, not how to prove, but how to express what they said. Whereas a Roman, in giving his testimony, was always jealous of himself, lest he should go too far; weighed all his words, and was afraid to let anything drop from him too hastily and passionately."[8] Or still, if we hesitate

[7] Juvenal iii, 77. It is amusing to see how Dr. Johnson adapted the lines to what was a corresponding prejudice, in his day not entirely unwarranted, against the French:

> "They sing, they dance, clean shoes, or cure a clap;
> All sciences a fasting Monsieur knows,
> And, bid him go to hell, to hell he goes."

[8] Abridged from Middleton's paraphrase, *Life of Cicero* I, 300, ed. 1741.

to take the Roman estimate of a conquered and subject people, there is the direct statement of Polybius,[9] himself a Greek, as to the slipperiness of the Greek character resulting from their rejection of the restraints of religion.

All this was involved in the difference between Socrates and the sophists; and unless we see clearly how the destiny of the Athenian people, and one might say of the world, was at stake, we shall make nonsense of the solemnity with which Socrates proclaimed his mission: "Therefore, O men of Athens, I am not concerned to plead for myself, as one might expect of me, but am rather pleading for you, lest by condemning me in your ignorance you throw away God's gift to you. . . . That I am really such an one given to the city by God, you may understand from my life; for it is not from merely human motives that I neglect my own affairs and see them going to waste these many years, while I look unweariedly to your interests, and come to you all individually, as if I were a father or an elder brother, with my message and persuasion of virtue." Such was the last public profession of Socrates, and it was not heard. This is not to say that the general decline of Greek civilization should be attributed to any special

Apology 30D

[9] *History* vi, 54, 55. See also the use made of this passage by Warburton in his *Divine Legation* I, 408.

class of men as the deliberate source of corruption. The serious corrupters of youth, to use the phrase of the indictment against Socrates, were not the sophists, as Plato himself admits, but the mass of the people, who were jealous of any distinction that ran counter to their own ideas, and made resistance to the course they were pursuing extremely difficult, even dangerous. The pity of it was that at this moment of intellectual curiosity and moral restlessness, when many generous minds here and there had caught glimpses of a higher law than tradition and needed to be encouraged in their quest of truth, the accredited teachers of the land should have disappointed the searchers and left them without any power of united resistance. The condemnation of the sophists, as a body, is not that they turned the current of thought in a new direction, but that they were themselves so deeply immersed in the popular tide, and lent their weight to its onward sweep.

Republic 492A

Unless this is true there is no meaning at all in those earlier Dialogues of Plato in which he attacks the rhetoric of the sophists as being no genuine art, but only one of the many branches of popular flattery, like cooking and the rest. When he wrote these Dialogues, the particular men with whom Socrates had contended were no longer living, but the evil they had fostered was

Gorgias *passim*

very much alive, was even growing daily more manifest to any one who looked beneath the surface of things. Hence the note of bitterness and occasionally of despondence in the writings of the one man who saw to the heart of the contrast between Socrates and the sophists, and, knowing he had failed to convert his own generation to the Socratic doctrine, did not know that he was establishing his doctrine for future ages as the indefectible source of philosophy, "than which no greater good has come or ever will come to mortal men."

Timaeus 47B

Out of the depths of his inner life Socrates had arrived at the conviction of three truths, two of which, scepticism and spiritual affirmation, were, as we have seen, intimately associated, while the third, the rationalistic identification of virtue and knowledge, stood in apparently unrelated isolation. It was the task of his successor to expound these theses in a way that should force their acceptance upon any man who looked honestly into his own breast, and to carry them up to a point at which they should all three meet in a single harmonious system of philosophy. I do not mean that Plato saw the task lying before him in this limited and systematic form: his mind was too elastic, and his outlook on life too crowded with images of men and their destinies, to be confined in any formula however large. I mean rather that these theses were his fundamental conviction, as they were of Socrates—the skeleton, so to speak, which, more or less concealed, gave shape and strength and coherence to all his thought. And we on our part, if we may borrow Plato's license in shifting a metaphor, we, who would "swim through such and so great a sea of words" as stretches before us in the Dialogues, can find no safer light to guide us than these three motives to philosophy which he himself took from his master.

Parmenides 137A

CHAPTER II

THE SOCRATIC QUEST

THE fidelity with which Plato brings out the threefold impulse of Socrates to philosophy is evidence in itself that the same motives were at work in his own mind. But they are equally manifest in passages from which the biographical element is entirely absent. The theoretical basis of his scepticism may be left until we take up the discussion of his attitude towards metaphysics; here it will be sufficient to call attention to the note of profound disillusion running all through his works, and growing stronger with his age. "The doings of men," he declares at the end of his life, "are not worthy of great seriousness, yet it is necessary to be serious; and this is our misfortune. . . . Men are for the most part puppets and little is their share of truth." Socrates, I think, would never have spoken in just that tone of bitterness, born of a longer and sadder knowledge; but Plato's words, nevertheless, spring from the same vein of sceptical irony as that which he had so

Laws 803B 804B

Symposium 216E

often seen his master display in common intercourse. So deeply ingrained is this note of doubt or hesitation in the Dialogues that the leaders of the Academy after Plato's death passed by an easy transition into a form of scepticism barely distinguishable from that of the followers of Pyrrho. These men, if we may accept the verdict[1] of a late critic, justified their position, in part, by Plato's own fondness for such terms as "the probable" (*to eikos*), thereby forcing his philosophy into accord with the teaching of the sophists—an irony of Fate comparable to that which brought about the condemnation of Socrates as a sophist.

As for spiritual affirmation, Plato's language is fairly exultant with the faith in righteousness as the one thing which a man may safely assert, against all appearances, to be always desirable. Even above his magnificent art of exposition and dialectic, his real power of persuasion, for those who have ears to hear, lies in the earnestness of this direct and unwavering affirmation. When Socrates, in gaol and awaiting the hour of execution, was urged by his dear friend Crito to bribe his way to liberty, he closed his memorable statement of the self-imposed obligations of duty with a simile borrowed from the experience of religious

[1] *Prolegomena* § 10. This treatise, whether by Olympiodorus or another, is by no means negligible for the modern student.

devotees. "These things," he said, "I seem to hear as the Corybantes think they hear the sound of flutes, and the echo of these words keeps up such a humming in my ears as quite to drown out any contrary arguments." So it is today with the understanding reader of the Platonic Dialogues: he is like one who has hearkened to the same incantation of magic flutes, the very memory of which is able to overpower all the distracting voices of the world. But Plato was not writing only for the *anima naturaliter Platonica*. As a teacher needing withal to maintain his doctrine logically against the attack of adversaries, he could not rest in a bare affirmation; he was bound to discover some authority for his faith, some definition of this higher knowledge, to which reason, if honest with itself, would at least willingly submit.

Crito 54D

Furthermore, the tendency to a positive rationalism was as strong in Plato as it was in Socrates. His belief in the simple identification of virtue and knowledge is constantly coming to the surface in his writings, and even in the *Laws* he is still reasoning on the familiar Socratic thesis that no man errs, or sins, willingly, but only through ignorance. Now, as I have said, such a maxim seems on its face to run counter to the known motives of human conduct, since any man, if questioned on his conduct, will admit that he often does

860D ff

wrong against the knowledge of what he knows to be best for him. Here, then, is an issue between philosophy and apparent fact; and if you solve this difficulty by explaining the equation of virtue and knowledge after the manner of the utilitarians, as Socrates in a manner did, you forthwith lay yourself open to the charge of throwing away your spiritual affirmation.

At the outset of his philosophical career Plato was thus beset with the double problem, first of justifying separately his rationalism and his higher intuition, and then of harmonizing these two seemingly contradictory positions. So far as we can conjecture from the records, Socrates himself had faced and solved the problem of rationalism raised by his identification of virtue and knowledge, and to this extent Plato, in writing his Dialogues, had only to repeat and clarify the steps of what may be called the Socratic Quest. But at this point Socrates ceased to be an expositor of his own philosophy: for the justification of spiritual insight before the bar of reason, which may be called the Platonic Quest, and for the relation of insight and rationalism, which had been left as the Socratic Paradox, Plato had to rely on his own resources of argument. Our study of Platonism, therefore, will follow this order: taking up first the Socratic Quest, we shall pass then to the Platonic Quest, and from these proceed to the Socratic Paradox. Or, expressed in the language of the three theses, our task is, first, to deal with the rationalistic identification of virtue and knowledge, secondly to see how scepticism leads from this thesis to spiritual affirmation, and, thirdly, to discover how this rationalism and affirmation can be held together.

Now, there is a group of Dialogues, almost certainly the earliest written, in which Plato is engaged in pursuing the Socratic Quest, as if lured on by a goal already clearly enough seen and within easy reach, yet at the same time with glimpses of another goal beyond, still wrapped in the haze of distance. None of these Dialogues is conclusive, and at the end of each the reader is left in a mood like that of the ancient Persian, who complained that he had heard great argument

> About it and about, but evermore
> Came out by the same door where in he went.

Meanwhile, however, these Dialogues wind in and out of their theme with such delightful ease, and gather by the way so many charming pictures of Athenian manners, that they might well be named the idylls of philosophy. Indeed, if I may confess my private taste, I almost at times hold them more precious than those greater Dialogues in which Plato no longer speaks as an inquirer but as a perfect master. For Truth, it may be, is to be worshipped at a distance, a creature so high and divine that no man, not even a Plato, can lay hands on her without a little soiling her robes. And these early Dialogues, as I assume them to be, have the peculiar fascination of suggesting the truth to us as something certain yet unapproached.

Each of them sets out to define a particular virtue—*Charmides* temperance, *Laches* bravery, *Euthyphro* holiness, *Lysis* friendship—and each ends by rejecting as inadequate or inconsistent the various proposed definitions. But through all their inconclusiveness, these two thoughts are continually before the mind: that in some way which the debaters cannot understand the different virtues are distinct from one another, yet at the same time merely aspects of one all-embracing virtue; and, secondly, that in some way, equally obscure to the debaters, this one inclusive virtue is dependent on knowledge.

A glance at one of these early Dialogues will indicate the character of all. In the *Charmides* we find a boy of this name presented by his elder cousin and guardian, Critias, to Socrates as a perfect specimen of that comeliness and grace and modesty, united with strength and self-mastery, which gave to the youth of that age and land their peculiarly androgynous charm. He is the embodiment of the much-lauded and much-desired virtue of *sôphrosynê,* which, for lack of a better equivalent, we translate "temperance." And Socrates, having introduced the topic by one of his dramatic ruses, proceeds to question the lad about this virtue, insinuating that he ought to be able to define it if it is really in his possession. Temperance, replies the boy, after some hesitation, is a way of doing things sedately, a kind of quietness or slowness in action. And so the discussion begins; for, in his usual manner, Socrates finds difficulties in this definition. Certainly, he says, and Charmides admits, temperance is one of the fair and excellent things (*tôn kalôn*); yet we should not bestow such epithets upon a person who learned his lesson or ran a race slowly, but upon one who was swift and agile. The lad, thus driven from his first definition, tries another: it is, he thinks, a kind of true shame or modesty. But again, objects Socrates, surely temperance is a good thing, as well as a fair thing, and, as Homer has declared, modesty is not always good for a man who is in need. And so once more the boy and his examiner seem to have reached a blind wall.

Now, a plain unimaginative man like Grote will see little profit in this sort of word-play beyond its tendency to shake the ignorant out of their confidence; and there is that in this first part of the Dialogue—and something more. It is an admirable example of the superficial sophistry to which Plato sometimes descends, whether wittingly or unwittingly, while the conclusion he has in view is perfectly sound. The fallacy lies in the ambiguous use of such words as "fair" and "good," which retain their practical popular sense as signifying this or that kind of profit from specific ways of acting, while they include also hints and admonitions of a deeper sense as touching the purpose underlying any specific act. All temperance is good? Yes. Then it follows, if goodness is such a thing, simple and indivisible, as it is becoming in Plato's rational system, that temperance is only goodness, and bravery is only goodness, and so with the other specific virtues. In a word there is only one morality, into which all the virtues are merged indistinguishably, and any attempt to define a virtue by the specific good it imparts will result in confusions and contradictions. But then virtue that cannot be defined or applied is rather an aerial commodity for this workaday world; and so, where are we? Of course Charmides might have retorted that he was employing the word "good" in one sense and his interlocutor in another; but this would have demanded a power of analysis quite beyond his years—a power, in fact, which his literary creator had not yet attained, or which he most artfully concealed.

At this point the argument of the *Charmides* takes another turn. At the secret suggestion of his cousin the lad asks Socrates what he has to say of this definition: "Temperance is doing one's own business." That sounds well; but it does not take Socrates long to bring out its inadequacy, for how can doing one's own business be temperance until a man first decides whether what he is doing is beneficial or the contrary? He might be doing himself an injury while thinking a certain act was his business, and, manifestly, it cannot be acting temperately to do one's self an injury. Before a man can be temperate, therefore, he must know himself and his business. Here Critias takes up the challenge, and avers that temperance is just the sort of knowledge implied in Socrates' queries: it is self-knowledge. Moreover, he has a divine sanction for this definition, and from a source that must appeal strongly to Socrates; for the God of Delphi who meets the worshipper at the threshold of the temple with the inscription "Know thyself" is not issuing a command, but pronouncing a salutation after the manner of our "Hail," "Be well," and to be well is the same as to be temperate. By his manner of salutation, therefore, the God is instructing us that to know one's self and to be well and to be temperate are all one and the same virtue. Thus, by an easy transition, we have the argument slipping from the question whether the virtues are all one to the question whether virtue, this particular virtue of temperance at least, is not identical with knowledge. Critias, in associating virtue with self-knowledge, might seem to have reached the goal of the quest, but he is soon thrown by Socrates into embarrassment because he is unable to analyse the ambiguity lurking in the word "knowledge" similar to that which entangled Charmides in the use of the "good."

Under the cross-questioning of Socrates this knowledge which Critias identifies with temperance proves to be, not the knowledge of anything definite, such as that which we obtain from sight or sound, but just a knowledge of knowledge and of ignorance. But where is the profit in this insubstantial sort of knowledge? How, for instance, shall the possessor of this knowledge be able to distinguish the pretender in medicine from the true physician? To do this he will have to know some of the marks of the physician's art, something about health and disease, and this is a very different sort of thing from the knowledge of knowledge, whatever that may mean. And so it is with temperance; if we define this virtue as knowledge, it must be knowledge of some specific way of profiting ourselves, and not that mere empty knowing that we know or do not know.

The argument is all a tangle, in which we have become involved by the treacherous words "goodness" and "knowledge." Yet we are left with a hint of the way of escape, given in the last beautiful address of Socrates to the youth whose virtue was the occasion of all this seeking and doubting: "I would advise you to regard me as a babbling fellow unable to reason anything out, and of yourself to believe that, as you are more temperate, so you are happier."

Simple as this last sentence may sound, it is pregnant with meaning. After the fruitless arguing forwards and backwards, it awakens in us the sensation of one who has been long wandering in a blind labyrinth, and suddenly comes upon an opening in the wall through which he descries lying before him a clear and spacious garden. So strong is this impression that we should be tempted to believe Plato had written the Dialogue deliberately as a puzzle, having in his hand all the while the clues not only of the Socratic Quest in which he is engaged, but of the larger Quest that is to follow, were it not for the two great arguments of the *Protagoras* and the *Gorgias*, which seem to come after the *Charmides* and its group in time and to represent the author as still searching.

Much of the *Protagoras* is like the debate of the earliest Dialogues, only wider in dramatic scope. The sophist who gives his name to the piece maintains that the virtues are separate. Being separate, they cannot be embraced under any single category such as knowledge, yet they can, he thinks, be imparted by instruction. Socrates holds that they are all a form of knowledge, and so not many but one; and as they are identical with knowledge, he would like to believe that they are teachable, but is troubled because he can find no teachers from whom you can learn them as you can acquire the various arts from practitioners. The two disputants are thus completely at cross-purposes, and the reader is likely to be vexed at their apparent stupidity in missing the occasions of coming to agreement. For example, Protagoras has been forced to admit that three of the virtues—justice, holiness, temperance—are at least pretty closely akin, being all reducible to wisdom, or knowledge; but he still clings to his theory that the fourth virtue, bravery, is quite apart from the others. Whereupon Socrates proceeds to show that bravery too can be reduced to knowledge; since, as a virtue, it should not be confused with the headlong impulse of the unthinking animal, and can be nothing more than wisdom regarding what is dangerous and what is not. At this point

Protagoras takes refuge in silence, and the discussion comes to an end. Yet how easy, the reader is likely to say to himself with some impatience, it would have been for Protagoras to retort: Very good, my dear teaser; no doubt bravery is dependent on knowledge, just as temperance and holiness are, but just observe your own addition —"regarding what is dangerous and what is not"; it is this very *regarding* that makes the virtues different *applications* of knowledge, and so not one but separate. The retort is easy; yet beware. Unless you have got clearly defined in your understanding this slippery thing called knowledge, your questioner will attack you from another side, and you will fall a victim to his cunning, as Protagoras had already fallen in trying to explain how the knowledge of virtue is imparted in instruction.

So far, then, we seem not to have escaped from the labyrinth of the group of Dialogues in which the *Charmides* is included. But there is one important addition to be noted. This you may know, said Socrates at the close of the *Charmides,* that you will be happier as you are more temperate. Now, in the *Protagoras* for the first time, Plato takes up this further identification of virtue and knowledge with the sum of pleasures which, in ordinary language, is named happiness. We cannot get away from this one fact, Socrates argues, that the feeling of pleasure is in itself good and that pain is in itself bad; hence we seem to have here a sure criterion of the rightness or wrongness of our acts, in the result—not, of course, the immediate consequence but the final result—as shown by the balance of pleasure and pain. Virtue is reduced to a pure hedonism (from *hêdonê*, pleasure), dependent on a man's ability to calculate and weigh his sensations present and future. If, therefore, men are to be persuaded to follow justice and holiness and temperance, they must be taught that such a course of life in its totality imparts more pleasure than the contrary course. The conclusion may be given in the excellent language of Bishop Berkeley's use of this argument to undermine the logic of those who make hedonism an excuse for vice:

"But Socrates, who was no country parson, suspected your men of pleasure were such through ignorance of the art of reckoning. It was his opinion (Plato in *Protagoras*) that rakes cannot reckon. And that for want of this skill they make wrong judgements about pleasure, on the right choice of which their happiness depends. To make a right computation, should you not consider all the faculties and all the kinds of pleasure, taking into your account the future as well as the present, and rating them all according to their true value? And all these points duly considered, will not Socrates seem to have had reason on his side, when he thought ignorance made rakes, and particularly their being ignorant of what he calls the science of more and less, greater and smaller, equality and comparison, that is to say of the art of computing?"[2]

Manifestly the argument has reached here a certain conclusion, the Socratic Quest has touched the goal. Virtue is an act which will result in the greater sum of pleasure, and he will be the virtuous man who has the knowledge that enables him to calculate the consequences of his conduct, and to strike a balance in the terms of sensation. Knowledge has been defined by the content of pleasure and pain, and by such a definition we can say that no man errs, or sins, willingly, but only through ignorance. This, apparently, is the form in which Socrates held his thesis, and it has maintained its position in the world to this day; since Bentham formulated the utilitarianism of the eighteenth century it may even be regarded as the dominant theory of ethics, however it may have disguised itself by various additions and verbal modifications. And, in a way, when combined, as it was in the teaching of Socrates, with another truth of an utterly different order, it contains a kernel of truth.

[2] *Alciphron* II, xviii, abridged.

But taken alone as complete in itself, as it is professed by the utilitarian and as it was expressed in the *Protagoras,* it certainly is inadequate, if not false.

What assurance is there that any man, by his own judgement or even by the collective experience of society, shall be able at any critical moment to foresee the long series of consequences that may follow a particular act, or shall be wise enough to determine coldly, amid the warm solicitations of present desire, where the remote balance of pleasure and pain will lie? Such a calculation is but a fumbling guide at best; unless fortified by a higher truth it is likely to bring us, indeed in the end it has invariably brought men, to the Pyrrhonic form of scepticism, which thrusts aside the uncertainties of the far future, and seeks for tranquillity in accepting with a kind of stoic Epicureanism the pleasure in sight as the only reality—

> Ah, take the cash, and let the credit go.

But that is not the scepticism of Socrates, nor is this the goal to which Plato's mind is moving with the steady sweep of tidal waters drawn onward by a celestial force. What is this thing called pleasure which we have so lightly accepted as the sole arbiter of life? That is the question agitated in the *Gorgias,* and never afterwards forgotten by Plato.

By a roundabout way the discussion of the *Gorgias* is brought at last to a sharp dispute between Callicles, on the one part, portrayed as a typical demagogue of the day, a man interested superficially in philosophical questions, but at heart an agnostic and egotist seeking for a life of pleasure through power, and, on the other part, Socrates, represented here as the customary ironist, but with new resources of sarcasm for those who try to humiliate him and of stirring appeal for those who will heed. The brief for pleasure, which in the *Protagoras* was held by Socrates, is now put into the mouth of Callicles, in order to demonstrate its insufficiency when carried to the logical end, while Socrates, as usual, is made the vehicle of Plato's expanding thought—*von Aenderungen zu höheren Aenderungen.*

This talk about temperance and righteousness, says Callicles, with a cynicism that reminds us of certain latter-day prophets, is all humbug:

491Eff

"The nobility and justice of nature, as I now tell you boldly, is really this, that a man who would live rightly should permit his desires to grow to the uttermost and not temper them by discipline; and when they have thus grown he should be able to serve them by reason of his courage and wisdom, and satisfy any longing that may arise. But this is impossible for the mob. Hence, for shame, they conceal their own impotence by blaming such men, and say that intemperance is a dishonourable thing, as I declared before, thus reducing the better natures to slavery. And, being incapable of satisfying their longing for pleasure, they praise temperance and justice, for their own lack of manhood. Suppose a man were born the son of a king, or were capable by his own nature of making himself a king or tyrant or ruler, what, in the name of truth, would be worse or more dishonourable than temperance or justice for such a man—for a man, I say, who, when he might enjoy the good things of life and there was no one to hinder, should bring in the common opinion and reason and censure of the mob as a master over himself? And would he not be a wretched creature if he were so subdued by the specious honour of justice and temperance as not to grant advantages to his friends over his enemies, in the city where he himself was ruling? No, Socrates, the truth is—and you profess yourself a votary of the truth—that luxury and intemperance and liberty, these, if they are supported, are virtue and happiness; the rest is fopperies, the unnatural conventions of society, idle chatter."

Very good, replies Socrates, we have got down to the real point at issue; and he proceeds to draw inferences from this definition of virtue in a way that causes his antagonist to squirm with indignation. If pleasure is all, and there is no criterion beyond it, what should hinder a man from indulging himself in practices which can scarcely be named, which, in fact, we do not name today? Nor was there anything unfair in so pressing the argument. We need only look at the actual life in Athens, or in the Italian cities of the Renaissance, to learn that it is perfectly possible for a man to gratify his lowest and vilest desires without losing that sense of pleasure which the hedonist makes his norm of conduct. These grosser pursuits cannot be rejected on the ground that a true calculation, so long as it confines itself to a purely quantitative estimation of pleasure and pain, finds them in the end on the wrong side of the ledger. Such a reckoning may save a man from excess; it will not teach him to renounce any pleasure in itself. Callicles is decent enough to admit that some pleasures are in themselves better than others, and having thus granted the existence of the good, or the honourable, as a standard outside of pleasures by which we may grade them, he has virtually given up his case.

It is at this point that Socrates utters his cry of ironical humility, "Alas! alas!"—as it were a prophetic note of triumph over the hosts of sophistry. That is one of the great moments of philosophy, the moment when we pass from the Socratic Quest to the Platonic Quest; and I never read the exclamation put into the mouth of Socrates, but I think of the shout of Achilles, when he came from his

499B

tent and stood by the trench, with the divine splendour radiating about him. The real battle was yet to come, but there was terror in the walls of Troy.

"Seeing, then," says Socrates, taking up the argument formally, "that we have agreed together, you and I, that there is such a thing as the good and such a thing as the pleasant, and that the pleasant is not the same as the good, and that each is acquired by a certain attention and mode of action, according as we set out after the pleasant or the good—but before I proceed, tell me whether you say yes or no to all this." And Callicles, like a man brought to bay, says yes. Whereupon Socrates returns to the points on which they had differed, and now, fortified by this concession of Callicles, pronounces the verdict and throws back the slurs of his antagonist in a way that has never failed to hearten good men against the slanders and insults of unscrupulous power:

507B "And so, Callicles, we come to this necessary conclusion, that the temperate man, being, as we have described him, just and brave and holy, is entirely good; and the good man must do well and honourably whatever he does, *and he who is doing well must be blessed and happy, and the bad man who is doing ill must be miserable*. . . . Well, then, either this argument of ours must be refuted, that men are made happy by the possession of temperance and justice, and miserable by the possession of evil, or, if the argument is true, we must regard the consequences. . . . We must consider whether you were right or wrong in your abusive taunts, to the effect that I am unable to defend myself or any of my friends or family, or to save them from the extremity of danger, being, like an outlaw, at the mercy of any one who chooses to buffet me on the ear, if I may repeat your insulting words, or to deprive me of my property, or banish from the city, or, worst of all, kill me. Such a state, you declare, is the most shameful a man can be in. But I say, as I have often said, and there is no reason why I should not say it again—I say, O Callicles, the most shameful thing is not to be buffeted on the ear unjustly, nor to have my face or purse cut; but it is a worse thing and more shameful to buffet me and slash me and mine unjustly, and to rob and abuse my body or my house. In a word, to do any injustice to me and mine is a worse thing and more shameful for the one who does the injustice than for me, the sufferer. This is the truth as it appeared to us in our former discussion, and is now made fast and bound, if I may use a bold metaphor, in proofs of iron and adamant. So at least it should seem; unless you, or some one more audacious than you, should succeed in arguing fairly against what I am now saying. For as for me, my word is always the same: that I do not know how these things are, but that of all the men

I have ever met, as now, no one has been able to say otherwise without making himself ridiculous."

Thus, after taking a fall out of one adversary and then another, Socrates is at liberty to profess his tremendous affirmation of the moral life, in a tone very different from that of the calculating argument employed with Protagoras. But observe the door by which he has finally slipped into this new region. Weigh the sentence italicized above, by which the passage has been made, for it is the keynote of Platonism, the despair of the petty logician, the joy of the initiated: "He who is doing well must be blessed and happy, and the bad man who is doing ill must be miserable."[3] Now on its face this is no argument at all, but a bit of outrageous sophistry turning on the ambiguity of a phrase. *To do well* in Greek means both *to prosper, be fortunate,* and *to act righteously, justly.*[4] Callicles would have been ready from the first to grant that *to do well* in the sense of *being fortunate* is *to be happy*—naturally; but if he now makes no objection to the other meaning, that *to do well* in the sense of *acting justly* is *to be happy,* it is because he has been browbeaten by Socrates

[3] Ὥστε πολλὴ ἀνάγκη . . . τὸν δ' εὖ πράττοντα μακάριόν τε καὶ εὐδαίμονα εἶναι, τὸν δὲ πονηρὸν καὶ κακῶς πράττοντα ἄθλιον.

[4] In the preceding debate with Polus the argument (474c ff) had taken a similar turn by means of the ambiguity of the word κακόν.

into a state of submissiveness. To understand the full scope of this silent admission we must briefly recapitulate the argument.

Callicles had begun by drawing a distinction between nature (*physis*) and tradition (*nomos*). Nature is what we know by our immediate individual sense, that is by natural feeling; tradition is what we have not learned from our individual experience, but accept as the opinion, or common sense, of mankind. Nature, he contends, tells us that happiness depends upon the amount of pleasure we can wring out of life, and not upon the means by which we obtain this pleasure; therefore, in nature, it is better to be unjust than to be just. Against this precept of nature the law of tradition, or common sense, that it is better to be just than to be unjust, has no weight for any one who is cognizant of the facts, since it is merely an opinion which we try to make prevail with others, for our own advantage and not at all for theirs. The problem of philosophy, therefore, unless it should be content with a brutal form of hedonism, was to confirm the authority of the popular verdict, and to prove that it is true also in nature.[5]

Socrates, as we have seen, takes hold of the distinction thus drawn, and so entangles Callicles in

[5] For this contrast of nature and common sense, or common opinion, see *Laws* 659D, 889E, *et passim*.

his logic that at last he is obliged to accede to a qualitative difference in pleasures and to a criterion of life apart from them and above them. So far the discussion is perfectly fair, and to this extent Callicles has been forced by sound reasoning to admit that the popular common-sense opinion is also true by the test of his own feelings. We do know for a fact that one pleasure is better, in the sense that we naturally call it more just, than another. But the next step, that our *happiness* depends on this new qualitative criterion, rather than the quantity of pleasure, is not argued at all; it is merely slipped through by a verbal ambiguity, owing to the bewilderment into which Callicles has been thrown. The phrase *doing well* merges together the two standards of nature and common sense—to be happy by prospering is a thesis of nature, whereas to be happy by acting justly is a thesis of common sense—and, however it was with Callicles, Plato should not have let this confusion pass without comment. But neither here nor anywhere else in the Dialogue does the author show himself aware of the fallacy. Instead of bringing evidence to prove that the common-sense view is also true by the experience of each individual man, he allows Socrates to maintain his position by the mere arm of an invincible scepticism: "So at least it should seem; unless you, or some one more audacious than you, should succeed in arguing fairly against what I am now saying. For as for me, my word is always the same, that I do not know how these things are, but that of all the men I have ever met, as now, no one has been able to say otherwise without making himself ridiculous."

It is something—a great thing, no doubt—to have raised the common opinion of mankind to the solemn utterance of a spiritual affirmation, supported by the powers of scepticism; but this is still not philosophy, however it may be the basis of philosophy. Common sense may be right, but so long as it cannot tell "how these things are," cannot, that is, give an account of itself dialectically, it is open to attack and discomfiture. Now, so far from being able to give an account of itself, common sense is painfully aware of its unaided inability to square its verdict with the visible facts of life, and is continually taking refuge in the expected reversals of an invisible world hereafter. It declares that the just man must prosper and be happy, and in this declaration it never wavers; yet it beholds everywhere the prizes of the race going to the strong and unscrupulous, and in its distress it prays to God for vengeance on the wicked and for help to the righteous. So it was not only in Greece but the world over; and so it is today. How marvellously, for example, the trust and despair of religion were combined in the Jewish Psalms, and how legitimately our worship has adapted those outcries to its sense of present defeat and future victory, any one may understand by reading the great sermon of Newman on the *Condition of the Members of the Christian Church.*

And this is precisely the position of Plato in the *Gorgias*. Beside the magnificent profession of Socrates that the just man is happy, he sets Callicles' picture of the just man as he may be actually seen on this earth, buffeted and scorned, unable to protect himself against the machinations of evil; and, beyond the quibble of a phrase, Plato has no positive logic to prove that Socrates, in this point, is right. Whether conscious or not of this defect in the argument, he turns for his vindication from philosophy to mythology, fleeing, like the Christian Church, to faith in the power of another world to make good the disharmony of this. The Dialogue concludes with an account of the pagan day of judgement, when the naked soul stands, with all its secrets revealed, before the tribunal of Aeacus and Radamanthys and Minos, and, as these pronounce, is sentenced to reward or punishment. "For this," Socrates says, "was the law [*nomos,* the divine ratification of *nomos* as common sense] concerning men under Cronus, and is now and always among the gods, that he who has passed through this life in justice and holiness goes after death to the Islands of the Blessed, there to dwell in perfect happiness beyond the range of evil, whereas he who has lived wickedly and atheistically departs to the prison-house of vengeance and judgement."

So far Plato has come in the Quest: he has shown that the popular view of morality has the sanction of religion, and that, if only the myth of future retribution be true, then certainly it is better, measured by the ordinary standard of happiness, to be just than to be unjust. But what if the myth be rejected? The effort to confirm this verdict philosophically, by an argument based on the immediate knowledge of men, here and now, will be the task of *The Republic*. If Plato succeeds in reaching this goal, then the ambiguity of the phrase by which Callicles in the *Gorgias* was tricked into acquiescence will prove to contain no fallacy, but the truth of philosophy as it is expressed by the instinctive common sense of mankind.

CHAPTER III

THE PLATONIC QUEST

THE *Republic* is the richest book of philosophy ever yet composed. In its wide scope there is scarcely an important question of human life that is not touched on; ethics, psychology, metaphysics, science, education, art, religion—everything is here. Impressed by this diversity of interests, the pedant has undertaken to analyse the work into separate treatises, written at different times; and the casual reader, in his bewilderment, is likely to ask himself whether the whole thing is not the random outpouring of a powerful but illogical brain, the creation, perhaps, of a poet who has taken up the ungrateful task of philosophizing. Yet, with all its variety, the better we know the Dialogue the more strongly we feel its organic unity; and, indeed, the thesis that never for a moment is lost from sight through all the divagations of reason and fancy, ought to be clear enough to any attentive student. It is proclaimed by the author categorically more than once, notably in the beginning of the eighth book, at one of the cardinal points of the argument, where he says his design was to set forth the various forms of government, with the corresponding characters of individual men, "in order that, having seen all 544A these, and having come to an agreement about the best man and the worst, we might learn whether or not the best man is the most happy and the worst man the most miserable."

Words could not state more plainly than these that the object of the Dialogue is to come to an understanding about that affirmation of Socrates in the *Gorgias* concerning happiness and virtue, which was there upheld by the force of sarcasm and ridicule, but is now to be confirmed by argument and by illustration of a positive sort.

Here the problem arises as to the relation of the Platonic Dialogues to one another. The solution depends primarily on the time of composition. If these works which we have considered as forming a propaedeutic to *The Republic* are comparatively late in order, following at least the *Phaedrus,* which an ancient tradition held to be the earliest of all the Dialogues, then Plato, of course, was merely playing a part in them. If, however, they are, as virtually all scholars hold today, the unriper products of his genius, then we have still to answer the question whether they display the candid gropings of a mind attempting to pass beyond the Socratic Quest, or were written purposely as a preparation, with the conclusion of *The Republic* already in view. The decision can rest only on subtle inference and on comparison with the procedure of other writers. My own opinion is that the *Charmides* (with its companion pieces) and the *Protagoras, Gorgias,* and *Republic* certainly follow one another in this chronological order. But I cannot believe that they were all planned together deliberately as one complete design; for that would be to grant to their author a comprehensiveness of intellect and a power of artistic restraint almost more than human. Nor can I admit that they are to be taken as purely occasional treatises with no continuous argument; for that is simply to write oneself down as incapable of reading philosophy. The only other explanation is to see in them the inevitable development of Plato's thought, and to suppose that in each case the larger theme of the Dialogue to succeed was floating vaguely before him, but was not yet worked out in logical form. And this, too, is the most interesting theory; for I doubt if literature affords any other example of a mind circling outwards from a single central impulse with quite such fateful regularity of pattern—and when we have followed these broadening rings to the utmost reach of our vision, it is as if they still moved onwards and outwards to some far-off invisible shore.

The first book of *The Republic* is frankly an introduction, in which Plato recapitulates the Quest so far as this had carried him hitherto. After a dramatic exposition of the *mise en scène* he leads Socrates and Polemarchus into a genial debate on the nature of justice, very much as temperance was discussed in the *Charmides,* and bravery and holiness and friendship in the other early Dialogues; and with the same inconclusive result. No tenable definition of justice is reached, but the inference is subtly suggested that in some way justice is merely one form of an all-embracing virtue, and that this master virtue is somehow dependent on knowledge.

At this point the amicable conversation is broken by the sophist Thrasymachus, as the gambolling of lambs might be interrupted by the advent of a wolf. As Callicles, in the *Gorgias,* was a rougher duplicate of Critias in the *Charmides,* so the present antagonist is still more turbulent—a veritable devil's advocate; and to the end of this book we have what is substantially a summary of the main dispute of the *Gorgias.* You two, exclaims Thrasymachus, are talking silly nonsense and indulging in a game of mutual flattery. When urged by Socrates to give his own definition of the virtue, he asserts insolently that justice is the interest of the stronger, and nothing more; and then, shifting the words to their popular sense and calling that injustice which in his view of life is really justice, he repeats the cynical theory of the day, which we have already heard from Callicles, and now in this latter age are hearing proclaimed as a novel doctrine by teachers of the Nietzschean type. My meaning, says Thrasymachus, will be clear if we take the extreme case of so-called injustice, and see how happy it renders a man in contrast with the miserable creatures who are subject to him and obey the slave-morality—the injustice of the tyrant who brings a whole city under his will and is able to provide for himself and his friends whatever good he desires. The truth of what I say, adds Thrasymachus, is proved by the fact that in their heart of hearts men envy and eulogize such a character; for in reality people give hard names to injustice not because they condemn the thing itself but because they are afraid of suffering under it. To this unreserved glorification of power Socrates has no difficulty in replying. The man who holds it right to make his own supremacy the law of conduct must first understand what his interest is, even in this crude form, so that mere strength is not sufficient but must be united with some sort of wisdom; and as soon as this element of wisdom is admitted, all kinds of considerations of man's higher nature force themselves upon us and make the identification of happiness with sheer power unthinkable.

The conclusion of the dispute is like that to which Socrates and Callicles came in the *Gorgias,* only with this important difference: in the present case Socrates admits that nothing has been finally decided. "The discussion," he says, at the end of the book, "has brought me no real knowledge; for while I do not know what justice in itself is, we shall scarcely know whether it happens to be a virtue or not, and whether he who possesses it is happy or not happy." And now, instead of cloaking this ignorance in the myth of a judgement to come, he will settle down with his friends to lay bare, if possible, the inmost nature of this thing they call justice, and to discover the source of their, or rather his, assurance that it is better to be just than unjust, better even, if needs be, to suffer the extremity of injustice than to do injustice. To this end they will strip justice of all the honours and rewards by which a man is lured to act contrary to his natural desires, and in contrast with this will draw the purest injustice, free of all the penalties imposed upon it from without. They will picture to themselves a man who pursues through life an undeviating course of justice, yet who shall appear to others to be acting unjustly; and by his side they will set up the man who, like the owner of the ring of invisibility, is able to satisfy all his evil propensities without detection. Furthermore, for the sake of argument, they will suppose that the juggling pardon-sellers actually have the power to buy off the vengeance of the gods, so that by the sacrifice of a little of his ill-gotten gains the unjust man can be assured of as fair a prospect after death as the just man. Then they may see whether, under such conditions as these, the just man is still happy and the unjust man unhappy. If this proves to be the case, it must be because justice in itself brings happiness and injustice misery. The novelty of such a procedure they fully recognize, for, as one of them observes, from the beginning of the world, so far as the records go, there never has been an attempt to denounce injustice and praise justice as they are in the soul, themselves the greatest possible evil and the greatest possible good, even if they are hidden from the eyes of men and gods.

How shall this mystery be laid bare, and who shall read the writing on the secret scroll of the human heart? For a while the little band of searchers is daunted by the task; and then Socrates thinks of a device. After all, the State is but man writ large; if, then, we are balked in discovering what we seek in the isolated soul, perhaps its operation will be traced more easily in the conduct of society. And so, for the rest of the Dialogue, the working of justice and injustice is regarded alternately as displayed in the individual and in the Republic.

To begin with the larger writing, Socrates suggests that the easiest way to track down the virtues of a city or State (the words were about synonymous to a Greek) will be to follow its progress genetically from its feeblest beginnings to its consummation as seen in a highly developed civilization. A little examination shows that this advance is by what we should call today the increasing division of labour, or by what was suggested in the *Charmides* as the source of the virtue named temperance, that is by the practice of each man doing his own business. Such a law must not be limited to the individual, holding the shoemaker to his last and the farmer to his plough, but must permeate the organization of society; it will divide the people as a whole into separate classes, each with its special function in the common life. Three great tasks the State has: to govern itself, to defend itself, and to nourish itself; and to these vital functions will correspond the main division of the people into rulers and soldiers and producers. Then, if our principle of organization be sound, the State will possess the various virtues according as each of these classes carries out its proper activity: it will be wise when the rulers perform their duty competently, brave when the soldiers defend their fellow citizens under the guidance of the rulers, temperate when the labourers, obeying the rulers and protected by the soldiers, are industrious and productive.[1] But we have not yet found the fourth of the cardinal virtues, the most important of all, justice. As there is no separate class left, this virtue must somehow be spread through the whole of society. What else can it be but that very law itself of doing one's own business, which is the efficient cause of organization and the force behind the specific virtues?

Now if the virtues of the single man are analogous to those of the State, it must be because the soul itself has faculties corresponding in their

[1] There is some confusion in Plato's conception of temperance as given in *The Republic*. Thus, at 432A, it is regarded, not as the special virtue of the productive class, but as extended through all three classes. On the other hand, such passages as 434C and 435B would seem to be meaningless unless temperance is limited to the productive class. Only by this restriction of temperance to the lowest element of the State and of the soul can it be separated from justice. So, certainly, Aristotle, with apparent reference to Plato, understood the matter (*e.g.*, *Topica* v, 6, 10). The confusion in Plato is owing to his occasional failure to distinguish between the division of the State into classes and of the soul into faculties.

functions with the three classes of society. Two such faculties, or modes of the soul's activity, are manifest at a glance: reason, answering to the ruling class, and desire, answering to the productive, acquisitive class. And the specific virtues of these faculties name themselves: a man is wise when reason governs his actions, temperate when his appetites are under subjection to reason. A third analogy Socrates finds in the faculty by which we feel anger, indignation, resentment, pride, superiority—the *thymos*, or *thymoeides,* as it is called in Greek by an untranslatable term. This, it should be observed, was not what we mean or think we understand by the "will"; for the will, if Plato had had any word of precisely this signification, would not have been accepted by him as a separate faculty or mode of activity. He would have agreed with Hobbes in regarding it as "the last appetite in deliberating," and would have admitted the conclusive statement of Jonathan Edwards, to the effect that "a man never, in any instance, wills anything contrary to his desires, or desires anything contrary to his will, . . . the will is always determined by the strongest motive." The *thymoeides,* then, is the seat of the personal emotions as distinguished from physical desires. It is at once, as an appetitive faculty, akin to the desires, and by its mental characteristics close to the reason; it lies between the two, like the soldier class between the governors and the producers, and its virtue like theirs is bravery, or courage.[2]

And so, as Socrates says, our dream is completed, and by a fable, for which we may thank the gods, we have been guided to the discovery of justice in the soul. For evidently that principle of attending to one's business which was the organizing force of society and the efficient cause of the civic virtues is a shadowy image of what we are 443c seeking. In very truth the justice of a man is like that of the State, save for this important difference, that it is not concerned with the division of labour in outer things, but with the conduct and

[2] The psychology of Plato for its purpose is sound and effective, and he was within his rights as a moralist when he threw it into relief by the great metaphor of the State. But the reader of *The Republic* should be warned that Plato's mental procedure was the reverse of his rhetorical method, and that his psychology really preceded his sociology. The division of the State into classes was made not so much for itself as for an illustration of the activities of the soul. As such it was an excellent device of rhetoric, even of logic; but Plato, it must be acknowledged, sometimes overstepped the proper limits of analogy. He did not always remember that the State is a collection of fundamental units, and not, like the soul, a unit with various forms of activity. There are in the State rulers and producers, and the distinguishing virtue of the former is wisdom, as temperance is of the latter; but these classes are composed of individuals each of whom possesses all the faculties. The neglect of this simple fact has led our "divine" philosopher now and then, as it has led modern sociologists, into strange and devious imaginings. His most ardent admirers will confess that, whereas he generally shows a profound intimacy with the intricacies of the individual soul, some of his theories of the State have a remote relation to the realities of human nature.

being of the soul itself. It is the power that holds the several elements of the soul each to the performance of its peculiar duty, and forbids meddling. By it a man first brings order into his own nature, becoming one with himself, and having his members tempered and harmonized like the chords of a lute that make one music of many notes. And then, when the peace of his inner life is established and he is master of himself, he will proceed to act, as he has occasion to act, whether in a matter of private business or public interest, in accordance with the law of justice within him, calling any act just which preserves the balance of his soul and cooperates with it, and declining as unjust anything that would contravene and mar his self-control.

Justice, in a word, might by its very definition be taken to denote the happier condition of the soul in precisely the same way as health of body is more desirable than disease. But a definition does not necessarily force conviction, and all that logic can do—though its importance in this respect must not be underestimated—is to clear away from before our eyes the obstacles thrown up by false reasoning, and then to bid us look at the truth as it stands naked and revealed. In the end the success of any moral appeal depends on the consent of the soul itself; for of what avail, as

Gorgias 472B

Socrates asked, are argument and definition unless the hearer in his very heart bears testimony to them? And there's the rub. Our life is woven of endless changing emotions, and few of us are capable of distinguishing the permanent from the transient effects of our acts, and of disentangling the threads of experience so as to say that we feel thus now because we then did so. To draw proper conclusions we need the help of one who is able to throw such a light into the soul and character of a man as shall make us see clearly into those dark places. The philosopher, therefore, who is concerned with something besides verbal triumphs has no other recourse than to turn to the power of the imagination; and so Plato will devote the eighth and ninth books of his Dialogue to unfolding such a "counterfeit presentment" of the various forms of government and of the corresponding characters as shall compel the most reluctant reader to say: This is the very truth of things as I myself have seen it—

> O Hamlet, speak no more;
> Thou turn'st mine eyes into my very soul.

The method of portraiture will be a union of history and psychology. It will undertake to exhibit the cities of Greece actually passing from one form of government to another—from aristocracy to timocracy, and from that to oligarchy and democracy, and last to that tyranny which was the perpetual menace of these small and factious States, and which was to close with the despotism of Alexander and the more enduring domination of Rome. And at the same time it will set forth the traits of human nature which lie behind these political changes as their cause and material; "for States are not things of stock or stone, but depend on the character of the men in them, which drags all else with it whatever way it inclines." Plato, writing when the forces of his people were at ebb, gave only the descending scale of governments, so that his picture to be complete would need to be balanced by a corresponding study of the ascending scale. It may be objected also that events in this world are not so regular in their progress as he has made them appear; yet it is none the less true that his generalizations from the short and confused annals of Greece are in the main quite amazingly confirmed by the larger sweep of history, and it is still more sadly true that a reflecting man can scarcely turn from Plato's account of the weaknesses inherent in the nature of democracy without a shudder of apprehension. To take from Plato's broadly composed narrative a few sentences indicating the cardinal points of what might be entitled the Tyrant's Progress must necessarily deprive the picture of

Republic 544D

its symmetry and its power of persuasion, but that is one of the disabilities we have to face in our attempt to dissect what is a living body of thought and no dead logic. The Dialogue itself remains untouched for those who will read it.

Now the just man in Plato's scheme is the aristocrat, he who has his centre of action in the reason, which is the best part of the soul. Such a man may find himself in a society governed by quite other ideals than his own, a city where contention is rife and the ambition to prevail over others is stronger than the determination to rule over one's self He will indeed live at peace with his own soul, content to serve the State as best he can for the unseen rewards of justice. But the son, unless by some divine chance he inherit his father's strength of character, will probably be moved by different considerations. The mother, perhaps, will feel herself humiliated because her husband is not distinguished among the magistrates of the city, but lives in quiet contempt of the brawling courts and contentious assemblies, with, it may be, the appearance of indifference to her own feuds and vanities. She will inveigh against this philosophical life to her son, and the friends and very servants of the house will join in the complaints, and will urge the boy to go down into the battle and contend with the world's weapons for the prizes that his talents merit. To these exhortations will be added the force of many examples and the voices of the market place, all telling him that those who mind their own business and follow too fine a sense of honour, after the manner of his father, are no better than simpletons—

> Honour! tut, a breath:
> There's no such thing in nature; a mere term
> Invented to awe fools.

Thus the education of the world lays hold of him, and he loses his best guardian, that divine gift of philosophy tempered with the love of pure beauty which alone dwelling in the soul is able to preserve it to the uttermost. He becomes a timocrat instead of an aristocrat, a man in whom the glory of success and the name of authority override the simple law of justice and of intrinsic honour. He is no longer ruled by reason, but by undue predominance of the sort of pride that belongs to the *thymoeides*, or spirited faculty.

To understand the next step it is first necessary to note that by oligarchy Plato meant what we are more likely to name plutocracy, that is to say, "a government resting on the valuation of property, in which all real power is in the hands of the rich." The individual character corresponding to this kind of State will arise when the son of a timocrat sees his father suddenly miscarry in some mag-

550c

nanimous project, striking against the prejudices of the city as a ship founders on a sunken reef, and losing both reputation and authority, perhaps even life. Then the son, observing the insecurity of such a public career, will turn his attention to the more tangible advantages of money, and will devote his energies to the amassing of wealth. He will eject reason and pride from their high places, and on the vacant throne of his soul will seat the concupiscent and covetous element, to which he will pay homage as if it were the Great King himself. In the ordinary transactions of business he will play the game so as, perhaps, to acquire the reputation of honest dealing—that, indeed, is within the scope of his ambition—but observe him when he has got hold of some trust for which he thinks he shall not be made to account, and you will see the rapacity of his nature. He may appear in the eyes of the world a very respectable sort of person, but there is no real health in him, nothing of the power and peace of a soul at one with itself. At the best his is but a sordid life, absorbed in the calculation of profit and loss, in which there is little room for the education of taste or for the pursuit of pleasure in its higher forms. The very absence of finer interests will permit the grovelling and sensual desires to gather strength within him, and these will be kept down only by the one masterful desire of increasing riches. He will be at war with himself, although the prudent element in him will still be in the ascendant.

From such a state the transition to the lower stage of democracy is clear and rapid. Suppose the son of one of these money-getters comes into the early possession of wealth without the discipline of acquisition; almost certainly he will be unsettled by vain conceits and puffed up by the flatteries of those who wish to prey upon him. He will be taught to regard modesty as merely simple; to ridicule temperance as unmanly; to despise moderation and thrift as vulgar and illiberal. Such old-fashioned traits will be thrust rudely out of doors, and into their place will troop all those passions which his father had suppressed—insolence and anarchy and waste and shamelessness—rushing in now like revellers flushed with drink and crowned with garlands. All pleasures and desires are the same to him without distinction. He lives from day to day as his appetites impel him, indulging now in wine and lewd luxuries, then drinking water only and dieting; going in now for physical training, then throwing up everything for a spell of listless loafing; making a pretense even of the philosophical life, or throwing himself into some political excitement, or trying his luck in some business venture, living always without law or plan or purpose, taking license for liberty, and ceaseless distraction for the pursuit of happiness. He is not one man, but many, the fit double of the democratic city.[3]

Last of all comes the tyrannical man, by an easy change. In the soul of each of us there dwell desires that are innocent and desires that are harmful; even in the good man the evil propensities are not extirpated, but only held in leash. This we can see in ourselves when, after some undue indulgence of appetite, we fall asleep and, in this relaxation of reason and habit, become the sport of fantastic and lawless visions. Then sometimes, in our dreams, the wild beast within us goes forth boldly to slake its lust, and there is no crime, no shameful act of incest or violence or unnatural passion, which it may not commit. Exactly like this is the condition of the tyrannical man. He has been brought up in a democratical family to a perfectly unrestrained life, which the flatterers about him dignify by the name of liberty. His father and true friends still retain some moderation and balance among the desires that draw the heart this way and that, but the baser sort who hang upon him discover the natural bent of his temper, and by humouring this raise it to be undisputed lord

[3] It is only fair to add that by democracy Plato meant the license of equalitarianism; his aristocratic State was really a democracy governing itself by respect for what is best in human nature.

of the household within him, as it were a huge and winged drone in the hive, maddening him with a kind of frenzy to which every lesser impulse is made subordinate. Then indeed License is crowned king, and sits as the disposer of his soul. What he desires, whether his master-passion be for money or women or power, he will have, though it involve the sacrifice of every other emotion or necessitate any crime against those nearest and dearest to him. He is not a human being, but a ravenous beast, or resembles a true man only as a man may seem to act in those hours of turbid dreaming when the soul is swept along by visions of abominable lust.

Such is the Tyrant's Progress as it is drawn in the eighth and ninth books of *The Republic,* frightful enough in this brief outline, almost overwhelming when read with all the realistic details painted in by the relentless hand of the artist. Question may arise as to the propriety of applying the names "aristocracy," "democracy," and the rest to the different stages of the degenerating State, and indeed the whole subject of Plato's sociology, in the sense of those terms, must, as I have said, be considered by itself. But of the reality of these various conditions in the life of society or of the individual, by whatever political names we designate them, there can be no doubt at all.

To take the two limits, with which we are the most concerned, as was Plato, we recognize immediately the man whose faculties are each, so to speak, attending to its own business—the man who is wise by the due exercise of reason, temperate by the proper control of his appetites, brave and self-respecting by the measured activity of the *thymoeides*; and who deals with the world as he deals with himself. And we know equally well the flimsy creature who is tossed about from one unstable passion to another, until he sinks to the still lower stage, when out of the conflict of unguarded desires one master-passion arises, like the criminal tyrant in a lawless State, to enslave the man's soul and drive him furiously across the rights of others.

Well, Plato may now ask, have I not made out the case for Socrates? No one can look at these contrasted portraits of the aristocrat and the tyrant without granting their veracity, or without saying to himself: "Yes, if this be justice, then the just man is in his own nature happy, and, if this be injustice, then the unjust man is in his own nature miserable. These equations correspond with what I have suspected in the lives of other men, and with what is the certain experience of my own life. It is no more possible to escape these conclusions than to deny that physical health means a state of pleasurable existence and disease means pain." This is the last and supreme *argumentum ad hominem:* It is *better* to do justice simply and solely because you are *happier* so doing than otherwise.[4]

Do we seem to have gone a long way round to reach at the last what was all the while near at hand? The conclusion is a commonplace, or to use a fitter term, it is the common sense of mankind, defended by the weapons of a terrible irony, confirmed by the insight of the man who perhaps saw more clearly than any one before him or after him into the obscure depths of the human heart, and made persuasive by the art of a masterly rhetorician. But there is this remarkable fact to observe about a true commonplace in the moral order: it passes current in the mouths of all unsophisticated men, yet if you question them about it you are likely to discover that they cannot explain its meaning, and if you press them closely you may even bring them to deny that it has any meaning. As for the commonplace which forms the goal of the Platonic Quest, it not only has these features of other commonplaces of morality, but it stands at the bifurcation of the road where religion and philosophy part company. Religion, though like

[4] Compare the last proposition of Spinoza's *Ethics*: Beatitudo non est virtutis praemium, sed ipsa virtus; nec eadem gaudemus, quia libidines coërcemus, sed contra quia eadem gaudemus, ideo libidines coërcere possumus.

philosophy it is really based on the Socratic affirmation, is yet too fearful to rest on this truth alone, and will seek another foundation for its faith in some miraculous event of history or in some revelation from above. So St. Paul argued to the Corinthians:

"Now if Christ be preached that He rose from the dead, how say some among you that there is no resurrection of the dead?"

"And if Christ be not risen, then is our preaching vain, and your faith is also vain."

"If in this life only we have hope in Christ, we are of all men most miserable."[5]

We are of all men most miserable—is not this the very reverse of what Plato thought philosophy was to teach when he set forth on his great search in *The Republic?*[6] I have not in mind to speak slightingly of the Christian faith, or of any genuine faith; I know the sources of religious conviction; but when I see the perplexity into which even St. Paul could be thrown by the fear of

[5] I Cor. xv, 12, 14, 19.

[6] With St. Paul's religious fear of scepticism one may compare the great passage of the *Apology* (40c–41D) in which Socrates states his philosophic faith as confirmed by the daemonic guide and undaunted by doubt: "To die must be one of two things: either the dead are as nothing and have no perception or feeling whatsoever, or else, as many believe, there is a change and migration of the soul from this world to another. . . . And ye too, my judges, ought to be of good hope towards death, being persuaded of this one truth at least, that no evil can befall a good man either in life or in death."

losing his belief in a particular miraculous event, I appreciate the force of Plato's boast that he alone, with his master, had the courage to rest his faith on the simple common sense of mankind. This is philosophy. Having expounded the meaning of the commonplace that it is better to be just than to be unjust, and having thus given authority to the affirmation of the spirit, philosophy does not seek for extraneous proofs of this truth, but proceeds to use it as a principle for investigating the manifold life and activities of the soul.

In the *Protagoras* we reached the goal of the Socratic Quest, when it was shown that the knowledge identified with virtue was the knowledge needed for the calculation of the consequences of any act in the terms of pleasure and pain. It now appears that the Platonic Quest has also brought us to knowledge, but to knowledge of a different order. To go back to our starting-point in the *Charmides,* it will be remembered that Critias suggested a definition of temperance, there the typical virtue, as the doing of one's business. To this suggestion Socrates replied that the endeavour to do one's own business would profit a man little unless he first had some knowledge of what business was really his own. And Critias, accepting the challenge, declared that temperance, or any other virtue, did presuppose knowledge, and was indeed such knowledge as the God of Delphi implied in the words "Know thyself," with which he greeted his worshippers in place of the ordinary salutation among men, "Rejoice." One feels, while reading the *Charmides*, that in Plato's eyes Critias had enounced a great truth, and that his subsequent entanglement by Socrates was owing to his inability to defend dialectically a sound position into which he had, so to speak, stumbled blindly. And now, in the appeal of *The Republic* to the inner experience of the hearer, we learn at last what was meant by connecting morality with the Delphic salutation. The knowledge commanded by the God is no empty "knowledge of knowledge," as it became to Critias under the fire of Socrates' questions, but receives a very definite content. To know myself is to be effectively conscious of this certain fact, that I am happy when I act morally, and, conversely, that I am acting morally so long as I am happy.

This knowledge of happiness is not of things future, nor is it, like the knowledge of pleasure, dependent for its authority on a fallible science of calculation; it is immediate and independent. Here, evidently, are two different orders of knowledge, on both of which our conduct is based, and Plato's philosophy has yet to explain the paradoxical bond between the knowledge which Socrates identified with virtue and the knowledge by which we confirm our spiritual affirmation.

CHAPTER IV

THE SOCRATIC PARADOX: THE DUALISM OF PLATO

THE conclusions of *The Republic,* it will be seen at a glance, are reached by a thorough-going dualism. In particular the criterion of happiness, whereon, as I think, the whole ethical system of Plato finally rests, will have no clear meaning for us unless we see how it came to be used by him as something essentially different in kind from pleasure.

In the *Protagoras* we heard Socrates arguing that, whatever else may be open to doubt, all pleasure in itself is certainly good and all pain evil. If on any occasion a man seems to reject a pleasure as evil, this is only because, if admitted, it would deprive him of a greater pleasure or result in an overbalance of pain. Therefore virtue is a science of mensuration applied to pleasure and pain; when we err in our conduct it is through lack of this kind of knowledge, and the common reproach that a man is overcome by pleasure is no condemnation of pleasure itself, but of the man who is in a state of ignorance regarding the most important matter of life.

This is the so-called philosophy of hedonism, or, if the phrase is not self-contradictory, individualistic utilitarianism. It probably, to judge from the way it was carried out in the Cyrenaic and Epicurean schools, represents a genuine aspect of the Socratic attempt to identify virtue and knowledge. But Plato, as we have seen, soon passed beyond that position, if indeed he was ever really satisfied with it. In the *Gorgias* he introduces Socrates as forcing his opponents to admit a seemingly qualitative difference in pleasures, and in so doing he virtually takes the foundation from under hedonism as a self-sufficient scheme of ethics. For the moment you grant a choice among pleasures not determined by the scientific mensuration of more and less, but based upon a qualitative criterion of good and bad, you are far along on the path towards admitting a criterion which is outside of and above pleasures and depends upon a generic distinction between all pleasure properly so-called and a feeling of another order.

The ruthlessness with which Plato at first applies this criterion would rather indicate that it was a new discovery with him and had not been in his mind when he wrote the *Protagoras*. Having perceived that pleasure, so far from affording the final measure of good, might even be contrary to the good, he seems for a while to have taken pleasure in denigrating pleasure. So, in the *Gorgias,* he outruns the requirements of his argument in forcing attention upon the disgusting possibilities of a hedonistic standard. Again, in the *Phaedo,* he recurs more definitely to the theme of the *Protagoras,* and repudiates its conclusions in the most vehement language. What are we to think, he asks, of those who, as the popular opinion holds, are brave because they are afraid to be cowards, casting out fear by fear, or of those who are temperate through calculation of future pains, masters of certain pleasures because they are the slaves of other pleasures? No, this is not the real business of morality, to barter pleasures for pleasures and pains against pains, the greater and the less, as if they were pieces of money. But that is the only right currency when we exchange all these things for wisdom and courage and justice, all these pleasures and pains for true virtue. Do you believe for a moment that the philosopher has any serious concern for these baubles that we call pleasures? They are but the poor affections of the body, whereas all the study of the philosopher is to escape, so far as mortal man can escape, from the body and its obscure interests into the

64D ff

world of Ideas which are the veritable life of the soul. The very intensity of a pleasure may be a hindrance to the soul in her labour of purgation and her search for the truth, since those things that cause us to feel most strongly are apt to seem clearest to us and truest, and so the keenest emotions may be those that bind us most closely to this earth. Every pleasure and every pain is, as it were, a nail that clamps the soul to the body and makes her corporeal, creating the opinion that those things are true which the body affirms, and preventing the soul from passing to the other world in her own purity and power. This is the tone, too, of the *Meno,* though less poetically coloured, and of parts of *The Republic,* and appears to represent Plato's middle period of lyrical revolt. At times he almost approaches the paradoxical enthusiasm of the first Cynic, who used to avow that he would rather go mad than feel pleasure.

But this unmitigated asceticism is a passing phase of Plato's philosophy and does not represent his final judgement of human life. In his later years he was to settle back into a saner attitude towards the common-sense view, and to recognize that pleasure was not in itself necessarily an evil, but mixed with good and bad, and, properly considered, one of the decisive guides of conduct.

Much of the *Philebus* is given up to a dispassionate analysis of pleasure and an endeavour to determine its relation to knowledge as the highest form of mortal activity. Still later, in the *Laws,* almost as if in a spirit of recantation for his earlier severity, he descends from his high philosophical scorn to discuss the quotidian uses of pleasure and pain as constituting the practical problem of education. These first books of the *Laws* are so frequently disregarded by writers on Platonism that it will be worth while to dwell at some length on their expression of his ripest and mellowest views.

In *The Republic* Plato had entered upon a discussion of the sort of education suitable for a citizen of the world, but had been turned away from his topic by the allurements of pure philosophy. After writing this Dialogue he went through what may be called a metaphysical period, and then, in his closing years, as life began to look less solemn to him, he seems to have felt doubts of the availability of his high morality for the common needs of mankind. And so the talk of the three friends, which forms the matter of his last work, will be "the temperate play of old men amusing themselves in regard to the laws." Instead of a debate on the uncompromising ideals of the philosopher, this Dialogue will deal with the educa-

Laws 685A

tion of the ordinary citizen and with the formation of a practical government.

The heart of the whole argument is in this notable passage of the first book: "We should consider that each of us as a living creature is but a divine puppet, whether created as a plaything of the gods or in some more serious mood. Of this we are not certain, but we know that the feelings [of pleasure and pain] are the sinews, or chords, that pull us in various directions." Hence the lawgiver who has to study the well-being of society cannot afford to neglect these motives of action; rather, his first object will be to get them into his own hands so as to be able to form and control the character of his citizens:

644D

"I say, therefore, that pleasure and pain are the original perception of children, and these are the things in which virtue and vice first come to the soul. As for wisdom and settled convictions of truth, fortunate is he to whom they come even in his old age, and he is the perfect man who possesses them with all their blessings. Now the virtue first appearing in children I call their education. If pleasure and liking, pain and hatred, are rightly implanted in the souls of those who have not yet learned to know them by reason, and if, when reason is added, their souls are in accord with it as to the fact that they have been rightly trained by suitable habits, this harmony is virtue in its completeness; but the part of virtue that has to do with the right training in pleasures and pains, teaching us to hate what we ought to hate from the beginning of life to the end, and to love what we ought to love,—if we separate this part in our discourse and call it education, we shall in my opinion be using the right name."[1]

The point to remember, then, is that to Plato's sober thought pleasure was not in itself a thing undesirable, nor yet in any way negligible (such a belief would have been simply inhuman), but was rather the most important matter to be considered in education from the earliest years of childhood. The health of the soul was involved, he thought, in the acquisition of right habits of feeling. At the same time it is clear that this healthy but unreasoning state of virtue ultimately was dependent upon something besides the mere difference between pleasure and pain; and, in fact, all through the first books of the *Laws* the education of youth is placed in the hands of men who have attained "wisdom and settled convictions of truth," and who are able to mould the habits of their pupils by the authority of "virtue in its completeness." The wisdom of these guides is the knowledge, as expressed in the conclusion of *The Republic,* that as we act morally we are

[1] I am not sure that my translation of this difficult passage is correct in every detail, but the general sense of the Greek is plain enough.

happy; their authority is in the fact that this feeling of happiness is of itself and always good, whereas pleasure is a subordinate feeling, to be controlled finally by a power outside of itself. In other words, Plato in the *Laws* has reverted from his temporary rejection of pleasure as intrinsically a snare of evil, but still adheres to his belief in the radical difference between pleasure and happiness, pain and misery.[2]

This most fundamental distinction of Plato's dualism is alluded to many times in the Dialogues, notably, and apparently first, in the *Gorgias,* where Socrates, to the amazement of his hearers, will not admit that the Great King, to whom every possible pleasure is open in the highest degree, is happy unless he is also just and righteous. In *The Republic* the same theme is taken up and elaborated in the strongest conceivable terms. For the sake of avoiding any misunderstanding two extreme types are isolated and contrasted one with the other. The unjust man is to possess all

470E

[2] I am fully aware of the ambiguity of "happiness" as a translation of Plato's εὐδαιμονία, but no better term seems to be available. "Eudaemony" is not English. The words "felicity" and "blessedness" suggest themselves, but are barred out by their association with a future life. I must beg the reader to divest the word "happiness" of the sense customarily given it in philosophy as meaning no more than a sum of pleasures, and to accept my use of it as signifying a feeling different in kind from pleasure. As a matter of fact this deeper meaning is often unconsciously, or half-consciously, conveyed by the word in ordinary speech.

the pleasures and so-called good things of the world, with unrestricted power to carry out his desires and with no prospect of coming pain to mar his enjoyment. Even beyond that, he is to have also the reputation of justice, so that the finer pleasures of honour shall fall to him as well as the grosser material pleasures. With his wealth he can even, as people suppose, make himself acceptable to the gods by the magnificence of his sacrifices. On the other side is set the just man, in his noble simplicity, the man who, as Aeschylus says, wishes to be and not to seem good. He is to possess his justice alone, without even the reputation of it, but, being the best of men, is to be reputed the worst. Let him be scourged and abused and cruelly tortured; let him know all the pains of existence and none of the pleasures, with no hope of compensation hereafter. Would Socrates dare to affirm that under such conditions the just man is still the happier and the unjust man the more miserable? And Socrates does not waver.

Nor does Plato waver.[8] In the matter of lan-

[8] This is true to the letter. But it must be admitted that nowhere in *The Republic* does Plato face the question in its most stringent form. Under normal conditions he portrays the just man as happy, and *vice versa;* but he does not demonstrate his hypothetical thesis that *the just man under torture with no expectation of a future life is happy.* His tacit neglect of this proposition places him almost in agreement with Aristotle's rejection of it as nonsense (*Eth. Nic.* 1153 b 20). This point had not been observed by me when the present volume was written, nor do I remember to have seen it

guage he may now and then fall into apparent ambiguities; for it must be remembered always that he had no technical terminology at his command, and employed words pretty much as they came to him. We should not therefore be surprised if at times, when the philosophical distinction is not the matter uppermost in his mind, he fails to discriminate sharply between the words pleasure (*hêdonê*) and happiness (*eudaimonia*), or even seems to take the latter consciously, in what was then, as now, its popular use, to mean merely pleasure in its larger and more stable aspect. There is, for instance, a curious passage of the *Laws* in which he begins by making the distinction clearly, as he had done in the *Gorgias* and *The Republic*, and then draws back from his position as if alarmed by its possible consequences. If, he says, the just life is not represented as offering also the greater sum of pleasure, and we force upon men the uncompromising question whether he is the happier who lives the justest life or he who lives the most pleasurable, why, they will retort upon us by asking what is the profit to your just man from his existence devoid of pleasure.

660E ff

made in any of Plato's commentators. I may add that this discovery was an important factor in bringing about a certain change in my attitude towards philosophy and religion. But the radical distinction between pleasure and happiness remains intact.—Note added to second edition.

Somehow, therefore, the lawgiver must refrain from separating the pleasurable and the just. He will say that we see these things but dimly, and so they appear differently to different men, just things appearing pleasant to the just man and unjust things unpleasant, but contrariwise to the unjust man. Now the judgement of the just man we must suppose to be more valid than that of the unjust man, and our task will be to make his judgement prevail as a criterion of pleasures. Such a conclusion might seem to carry us back to the abandoned position of the *Protagoras;* yet even here a phrase slips in which shows that Plato was merely arguing on a lower plane for practical purposes. This belief that the balance of pleasure belongs to righteousness is perhaps only a salu- 663D tary illusion, he says, which the cunning lawgiver can implant in the minds of the young, similar to the myths of the gods with which religion is bound up in the popular creed. Plato, in other words, was here writing for practical men and making his appeal to the ordinary intelligence. He saw that for such minds it would be useless, if not actually prejudicial, to present his thesis in the absolute terms of philosophy; just as the preacher today who is engaged in the cure of souls would probably succeed only in rendering religion fantastic or repugnant to sober people of the world by describing the agonies of a martyr at the stake and trying to make his audience realize that it is possible amid such torture to die in an ecstasy of happiness. Such a preacher would be proclaiming a psychological fact, but it is doubtful whether his words would be for edification.

So, I take it, there is a certain philosophical "economy" here and there in the language of the *Laws;* possibly, too, Plato's own naked conviction seemed to him in his later years, not less true, but less urgent for the common need of mankind. However that be, one thing is indubitable: he who has not grasped this distinction in kind between happiness and pleasure will wander in the labyrinth of Plato's Dialogues with no clue to guide him. He may admire their various beauties and their infinite riches, but they will be to him a maze without ultimate plan or exit.

This dualism of feeling, as I have said before and must say again, is the great discovery of Plato; its vital importance is proved by the course of philosophy among writers of the modern world who have forgotten it or tried in one way and another to avoid it. Certainly the history of ethical theory ought to establish one fact incontestably: no doctrine can speak with the peremptory voice of truth which eschews all forms of reward and penalty. No statement of a categorical imperative, no trust in an innate sense of duty, no exhortation to the love of God or of man, will avail against the temptations of the world unless the admonition bears with it the promise of satisfying what all men instinctively crave. The heart of man naturally demands pleasure or happiness, and will not forgo its demand.[4]

On the other hand those who have understood this trait of human nature, without admitting, tacitly it may be, the radical dualism of pleasure and happiness, have fallen invariably into one of two difficulties: either they have sunk into a degrading form of Epicureanism, or, shunning this error, they have lost themselves in the pursuit of elusive shadows. These difficulties are abundantly evident in the development of English utilitarianism. The strength of Bentham's system—and it had undoubted strength—lay in his steady perception of the relation between the practice and the reward of virtue. But his purely quantitative standard of pleasures left out of the account too large a part of human nature to satisfy the finer minds even among his followers. So we see John Stuart Mill endeavouring to abide by the half-truth of utilitarianism while giving to it a colour

[4] Those who think that happiness is omitted from the Buddhist scheme of salvation have strangely misread the books or, more probably, have not read them at all.

and a tone which should raise it out of the sty. "When thus attacked," he says, "the Epicureans have always answered, that it is not they, but their accusers, who represent human nature in a degrading light; since the accusation supposes human beings to be capable of no pleasures except those of which swine are capable. . . . It must be admitted, however, that utilitarian writers in general have placed the superiority of mental over bodily pleasures chiefly in the greater permanency, safety, uncostliness, &c., of the former—that is, in their circumstantial advantages rather than in their intrinsic nature. And on all these points utilitarians have fully proved their case; but they might have taken the other, and, as it may be called, higher ground, with entire consistency. It is quite compatible with the principle of utility to recognize the fact, that some *kinds* of pleasure are more desirable and more valuable than others. It would be absurd that while, in estimating all other things, quality is considered as well as quantity, the estimation of pleasures should be supposed to depend on quantity alone."[5]

Betham had recognized no difference at all between pleasure and happiness. Mill, by his addition of a qualitative standard, was really feeling his way towards a standard of morality above

[5] *Utilitarianism*, chap. ii.

pleasure, while still verbally denying the existence of such a standard.[6] He is the example *par excellence* of a philosopher who combines the most lucid powers of exposition with an incapacity of clear thinking. The entanglement of Mill and the later utilitarians was patent to T. H. Green, who sought a way of escape by saving desire as a motive of action while changing the object of desire. To this end he sets up a distinction between pleasure and what he calls "self-satisfaction," and argues that the object of our desire is not pleasure or even the pleasure of self-satisfaction, but is this self-satisfaction for its own sake, while pleasure, if it comes, is a mere contingent effect. By this analysis of the object of desire he thinks he has pointed to the source of Mill's confusion and has established a criterion of values superior to pleasure. Now many of Green's pages devoted to the elucidation and expansion of his idea of self-satisfaction are rich with the burden of history, and there is a hearty kernel of truth in his argu-

[6] Surely there is no consistency, but inconsistency, in the two members of Mill's sentence: "On all these points utilitarians have fully proved their case; but they might have taken the other, and, as it might be called, higher ground, with entire consistency." If the utilitarians are right in making "permanency, safety," etc., the standard of value and desirability among pleasures, what is the need or meaning of another, qualitative standard?—I admit freely that this question of a qualitative and quantitative standard of pleasures is extremely subtle, and for its complete answer, in accordance with the Platonic philosophy, should be deferred until after the consideration of Plato's psychology and cosmology.

ment. But there are two fatal weaknesses. In the first place Green's notion that *self*-satisfaction may consist in the sacrifice of the individual's well-being for the well-being of society is only Bentham's old fallacy, decked out in new terms, of supposing that we can appeal to pleasure as the motive of conduct and then avoid the egotistic consequences of such a creed by merging pleasure in the greatest happiness (as the utilitarians use the word) of the greatest number. And, secondly, Green is blind to the fact that, by rejecting pleasure as his motive while yet failing to find the criterion of self-satisfaction in happiness as a feeling distinct in kind from pleasure, he leaves his standard of self-satisfaction—so long as he writes consistently—without verifiable meaning or content. Take one of his typical sections:

. . . "To the question, What is the well-being which in a calm hour we desire but a succession of pleasures? we reply as follows. The ground of this desire is a demand for an abiding satisfaction of an abiding self. In a succession of pleasures there can be no such satisfaction, nor in the longest prolongation of the succession any nearer approach to it than in the first pleasure enjoyed. If a man, therefore, under the influence of the spiritual demand described, were to seek any succession of pleasures as that which would satisfy the demand, he would be under a delusion. Such a delusion may be possible, but we are not to suppose that it takes place because many persons, through a mistaken analysis of their inner experience, affirm that they have no idea of well-being but as a succession of pleasures."[7]

How often, while reading such passages as these, we feel that Green is on the verge of making the great discovery made by Plato so long ago, but is held back by the age-old fallacy of regarding happiness, or whatever you choose to call it, as nothing more than a succession or consummation of pleasures! What vain circumlocutions his noble spirit would have been spared, and what hair-splitting subtleties of argument, if he had been able to say in simple, straightforward language, "This self-satisfaction or well-being which I am trying so hard to offer as a substitute for the unsatisfaction of pleasure is just the happiness that every man has felt and may understand!"[8]

No, mankind craves happiness; it can be weaned from the seduction of false pleasures only by this possession which is so like pleasure yet greater and essentially other than pleasure, and it will be diverted by no empty promises or threats. The whole religious literature of the world, truer

[7] *Prolegomena* § 234.

[8] The distinction between pleasure and happiness is implicit in such passages of the *Prolegomena* as §§ 228, 238; but it is never defined or brought out into the light, and for the most part Green accepts happiness in the utilitarian sense as the sum of pleasures.

in its candid reliance on the intuitive knowledge of the soul than are the rebellious searchings of the schools, is replete with appeals to our consciousness of the difference between pleasure and the rapture, or peace, or happiness—the word is nought but the fact is everything—of obedience to a higher law than our personal or physical desires. I could cover many pages with passages to this effect; a single quotation from one of the older of our English divines, the length of which may be excused by the importance of the topic, will suffice:

"That joy should be enjoined, that sadness should be prohibited, may it not be a plausible exception against such a precept, that it is superfluous and needless, seeing all the endeavours of men do aim at nothing else but to procure joy and eschew sorrow; seeing all men do conspire in opinion with Solomon, that *a man hath nothing better under the sun than—to be merry.*

"It is true that men, after a confused manner, are very eager in the quest, and earnest in the pursuit of joy; they rove through all the forests of creatures, and beat every bush of nature for it, hoping to catch it either in natural endowments and improvements of soul, or in the gifts of fortune, or in the acquists of industry; in temporal possessions, in sensual enjoyments, in ludicrous divertisements and amusements of fancy; so each in his way doth incessantly prog for joy; but all much in vain, or without any considerable success; finding at most, instead of it, some faint shadows, or transitory flashes of pleasure, the which, depending on causes very contingent and mutable, residing in a frail temper of fluid humours of the body, consisting in slight touches upon the organs of sense, in frisks of the corporeal spirits or in fumes and vapours twitching the imagination, do soon flag and expire.

"Wherefore there is ground more than enough, that we should be put to seek for a true, substantial, and consistent joy. It is a scandalous misprision, vulgarly admitted, concerning religion, that it is altogether sullen and sour. Such, indeed, is the transcendent goodness of our God, that he maketh our delight to be our duty, and our sorrow to be our sin, adapting his holy will to our principal instinct; that he would have us to resemble himself, as in all other perfections, so in a constant state of happiness. Indeed, to exercise piety and to rejoice are the same things, or things so interwoven that nothing can disjoin them."[9]

It is the honour of Plato that he sought to establish this fundamental truth of religion by basing it on the immediate intuition of the mind, even apart from any recourse to the problematical rewards and penalties of another state of existence.

This is the beginning of Plato's dualism, but

[9] From the forty-third sermon of Isaac Barrow, with omissions.

not the end. If happiness and pleasure are distinct feelings, it will follow that the activities they accompany, or the motives of our activity, are likewise distinguished in kind. We are brought back to that troublesome and recurring question of the early Dialogues as to the identity or separateness of the virtues. Somehow it appeared there, as we took up bravery and temperance and holiness in turn, that they all had a tendency to run together into one supreme virtue; yet, as soon as we reached this point, invariably the particular virtue under discussion lost its concrete value, and we were left with an empty word on our hands which had no significance for solving the specific problems of life. Now, if we return to these unanswered puzzles after considering Plato's later Dialogues, we shall see that the difficulty lay in the ambiguity of the word "virtue" (*aretê*), which is used for two quite different things. For our own convenience, therefore, we will henceforth make a distinction in language which Plato himself never made, by using different translations for the same word to denote a distinction in fact which he did make. So far as possible we will reserve the word "virtue" for the art of living, for right conduct, that is, as manifested in specific spheres of activity, and will adopt the word "morality" for the higher unity in which the particular virtues seemed to have a way of losing themselves.

It is not easy to decide how fully Plato himself in his earlier Dialogues was aware of this distinction which later becomes so important to his ethical system. In the *Protagoras* it is latent. We can see it growing clearer in the *Phaedo* and the *Meno,* though it is there still only implicit. In *The Republic* the distinction is something more than implied by the separate treatment of the group of virtues—wisdom, bravery, temperance—on the one hand and of justice on the other. Wisdom is the right action of our reason, bravery of the *thymoeides,* and temperance of the desires. These are the specific virtues. Justice is the compelling and governing force behind all these forms of activity, the healthy balance of the soul as a whole and its right energy as a unit. This distinction between morality as the central governing force and the virtues as specific forms of activity is brought out even more clearly in the *Politicus,* where it is shown that the specific virtues, or perhaps we should say the tendencies that create them, may come, if left to themselves, into actual conflict one with another. Thus, for example, bravery and temperance are not only different one from the other, but may take hostile sides in the soul of a man or in a State. Bravery, in so far as it is the

306A ff

quality of a temperament quick and virile by nature, is apt, if unrestrained, to run into impetuosity and insolence; whereas temperance, as it is found in a disposition inclined to slowness and quiet, may very easily sink into sloth and cowardliness. These temperaments and virtues manifest themselves in two classes of men who may divide a city into factious parties (Plato would say today into radicals and conservatives), and whom it is the art of the true statesman to reconcile in friendly co-operation for the common good. Though Plato does not here draw the parallel out in so many words, it is everywhere implied that this royal art (*basilikê technê*) of the governing statesman is but another name for justice, equivalent to the moral principle that in the individual soul resides above the various activities, and governs and harmonizes the specific virtues.

But for the final exposition of this, as of so many other doctrines, we must turn to the book of Plato's old age. All our laws, he says at the conclusion of that long treatise, must be controlled by some one purpose. As the physician has a definite end in view, the preservation of health, to which all his activities are directed, and as the pilot has a definite task, so it must be with the statesman, or lawgiver. The aim of the statesman is the creation and preservation of virtue in the

Laws 963A ff

State; and as his aim is thus not many, but one, so the virtues which have appeared to us all along as fourfold must also in some way be one virtue, or subordinate to some one moral purpose. It was easy to see what was meant by the special virtue of bravery; it is a manner of facing things fearful. The nature of wisdom, too, is clear; it is a kind of prudence in the choice and use of means. And in the same way we understand temperance and justice. But what is the character of the moral force in subservience to which these various virtues are united? It is a kind of wisdom—not prudence, but the mind, or intelligence—working in him who is able not only to discern the many different activities of life but to look beyond them; the divine vision of him who, whatever may be the field of observation, is able to behold the changeless law above all change. It is the knowledge, religiously speaking, of the gods, that they are and that they govern the world by a beneficent design. There are two ways by which we may approach this supreme knowledge: one by the soul's perception of her own nature, that she is the oldest and most divine of existing things, lord of the body by right of age and dignity; the other by the perception of the ordered motion of the stars and of all created objects that display the governance of an omniscient intelligence; and these two ways are virtually one. He will be a true worshipper of the gods who has attained to this knowledge of the soul's hegemony and of the indwelling reason of the universe. He alone possesses that saving morality (*aretê sôtêrias*) which fits him to be the ruler of himself and of the State.[10] 969c

Such, freely and succinctly rendered, but I think not misinterpreted, is the ethical position of Plato in the conclusion of the *Laws* and at the end of his life. Substantially it is the same as the doctrine of *The Republic*, though the terminology is different. In both Dialogues there are four virtues, one of which is taken—with some confusion of thought, it must be admitted—now as parallel with the others, and now as distinct from them by reason of its quality of leadership and comprehensiveness. *The Republic* gave the double function to justice; in the *Laws* justice tends to be limited to the political virtue of right distribution, whereas the moral leadership is transferred to the reason, in such a way that wisdom is treated both as one of the four cardinal virtues and as the queen over them all. Evidently this ambiguous

10 Philo Judaeus, in his *Legum Allegoria* (I, 63ff.) has a quaint comparison of the ἀρετὴ γενική, as he calls the super-virtue, and the four ἀρεταὶ κατὰ μέρος with the river that went out of Eden to water the garden, and from thence was parted, and became into four heads. The doctrine is Stoic and Christian as well as Platonic. See, for instance, Stobaeus, *Ethica* VI, i; Maximus Tyrius xxvii; Chrysostom, *In Mat.*, 189B; Clem. Alex., *Strom.*, I, xx, 99.

position of wisdom is explained by the fact that we are dealing with two kinds of knowledge, and points to a further dualism of Plato's philosophy.

Along with the question of the unity and diversity of the virtues there ran through all the early Dialogues another problem, which was left in an equally unsettled state. The morality, or super-virtue, into which the specific virtues had a fashion of merging and so escaping our search, was always some kind of wisdom or knowledge. Bravery, so soon as it became a desirable quality and no mere impetuosity of temper, involved a knowledge of what things are properly to be feared and what are not. Temperance was meaningless until we acquired an understanding of ourselves and of what was good for us. It would follow that, if all these forms of virtue rest on a body of knowledge, they ought to be teachable, like medicine or any other art; yet in practice there seem to be no teachers to whom a man can go to learn morality as he can go to a physician to learn medicine. This paradox reached its climax in the *Protagoras,* where Socrates argued that theoretically all the virtues are knowledge yet practically are not teachable, while his antagonist held that the virtues have each their individual character apart from knowledge yet can be taught.

It now appears that this paradox lay in the

ambiguity of a word; and in the later Dialogues, whatever may be said of the other aspects of Plato's philosophy, the double character of the relation of the mind to facts is brought out with a precision and dwelt on with a persistence which leave no doubt of his fundamental dualism. In *The Republic* the distinction is represented pictorially by the bifurcated line, separating knowledge proper from what is properly called opinion; and thereafter these two terms are employed regularly for the two processes that caused the earlier ambiguity. The full bearing of this terminology on Plato's system must be left for another chapter. Here the point to observe is that the primary motive for making the distinction is rather ethical than metaphysical, as may be seen from the trend of the argument in the *Theaetetus*.

The avowed purpose of this Dialogue is to determine whether knowledge and perception (*epistêmê* and *aisthêsis*) are the same thing or different things; to discover, that is, whether we have any fixed and certain form of knowledge. But this thesis soon becomes involved with the subsidiary questions whether all things are in a state of flux and whether man is the measure of all things. Twice at least these three problems are brought together quite definitely, but for the most part the discussion passes from one to another of them

163A

160D
168B

after the rather disconcerting manner sometimes adopted by Plato. The best clue to guide the reader through this labyrinth is a sense of what was the dominating interest in the author's mind; nor is this interest hard to discover. Here, as almost everywhere in Plato, the bias is ethical; 157D the real animus of the Dialogue is the desire to demolish the belief, shared by the sophists with their audiences, that there is no certain reality behind our sense of the good and the beautiful. And so, in a way, the process of proving is inverted: if this stronghold of popular unreason is undermined, then the answers to the three troublesome questions will follow of themselves. If you grant the existence of a principle of goodness, fixed and immutable, then there is a standard of values fixed, there is something besides the flux, there is a knowledge superior to that depending on outer perception (which Plato will grant to the flux), and man, in the Protagorean sense, is not the measure of all things.

To this end the arch-sophist Protagoras is brought to the bar, and under the cross-questioning of Socrates is forced to admit the inclusion of a standard of "better" and "worse" in our judgements. But, while making this admission, he still clings to his dogma that man (that is, always, man as a creature totally immersed in the flux) is the measure of all things; he still maintains that as things seem just and beautiful to each State, such they are as long as the State so judges them. Socrates retorts with the argument that, if there is no objective and fixed reality in the moral world, no standard by which the degrees of better and worse can be determined, then the use of such words as "just" and "beautiful" is perfectly meaningless—a conclusion against which our common sense revolts implacably. Furthermore, though a man may assert that the just is whatever a State regards as better for itself in the sense of being more profitable, yet no one will say, unless he is merely amusing himself with words, that whatever a State regards as profitable, and so establishes as the law of justice, will necessarily turn out to be profitable in the event. This introduces the question of the future, and shows that at least the profitable is not measured by the present opinions of men (in other words, that to this extent man is not the measure), and that probably the justice which the sophists are so fond of connecting with profit may also be something uncontrolled by opinion—something about which it very much behooves a man to get not opinion but knowledge.

167C

177D

But is there any such thing as knowledge? How shall we take it as a guide unless we know what it is? Plato has no answer to this question put as a problem of epistemology. We cannot, he de- 209E clares, get at a knowledge of what knowledge is by analysing the process of knowing, for the reason that this analysis implies knowledge of the 196D parts, and so on *ad infinitum*. And again he asks, as might be asked of any one, ancient or modern, who thinks the tantalizing problem of epistemology has been solved, whether perhaps it was not a bit impudent ever to have supposed they were going to define the process of knowing when they did not know what knowledge is.[11] It is characteristic of Plato, however, that he does not deny the possibility of defining knowledge in the terms of the intellect, but only confesses the failure on this occasion to reach such a definition. He will not step beyond the bounds of Socratic scepticism: so far, he says, using Socrates as his mouthpiece, 210C and no further my art prevails, to clarify the mind of the docile listener and make him more agreeable to his friends.

But with this sceptical outcome as regards the avowed epistemological issue, the Dialogue contains two statements, one dropped casually by the way, the other uttered with all the impressiveness at Plato's command, which permit us to see what

[11] For Plato's scepticism in regard to epistemology see also *Charmides* 169A.

positive answer Plato had in reserve. The former occurs in connection with a rather whimsical account of the aboriginal irrational elements underlying phenomena, which can be named but of which nothing can be predicated, and suggests that there may be similar elements of sensation in the soul, in regard to which the soul may be in a state of truth, although it cannot be said to know them, since knowledge comes only with rational discourse.[12] The other, and more explicit, statement is made in the digression on the philosophic life, which, to one not familiar with Plato's indirect methods, might appear to be strangely out of place in the heart of this Dialogue. Our only refuge from the evils of this world, says Socrates, is to render ourselves like unto God. In him there is no injustice, no shadow of wrong, but, as we conceive things, purest justice; and there is nothing that more resembles God than he among us who becomes as just as it is possible for man to be. The knowledge (*gnôsis,* superrational intuition) of this truth is wisdom and morality, and the

202B

176B

12 This passage of the *Theaetetus* is, I admit, obscure. My interpretation of it would be confirmed by a sentence of the *Philebus* (66c), as read by Ficino: Πέμπτας τοίνυν, ἃς ἡδονὰς ἔθεμεν ἀλύπους, ὁρισάμενοι, καθαρὰς ἐπονομάσαντες τῆς ψυχῆς αὐτῆς ἐπιστήμας, ταῖς δὲ αἰσθήσεσιν ἑπομένας —*puras nominantes animae ipsius scientias, sensus autem sequentes*. Compare also *Timaeus* 52B and Plotinus II, iv, 10. But however this passage of the *Theaetetus* be taken, there is no possibility of misunderstanding the words in which Plato affirms the reality of the superrational intuition.

ignorance of this truth is folly and manifest evil; and all other seeming wisdom is comparatively a vulgar and mean thing.

The *Theaetetus,* so analysed, bears throughout on the question now under consideration. Leaving aside as doubtful and, for the present purpose, relatively unimportant the suggestion of an infrarational intuition of immediate sensation, we have these two conclusions: an admission of the practical impossibility of discovering any definition of knowledge regarded as the relation of human reason to objective facts, and an affirmation of the higher intuition, which is above reason and is true knowledge. The gist of the argument is the opposition between the Platonic dualism of knowledge and opinion and the Protagorean (and, in general, the sophistic) monism. Plato does not deny that men move about in a world of shifting impressions, and are constrained to base their conduct on judgements drawn from observation of facts which never can be complete; in our practical life, so far as it is concerned with phenomena, we have only the guidance of opinion. To this extent he agrees with Protagoras, though even here he draws ethical conclusions very different from those of the sophist; but he does deny flatly the Protagorean dogma that this shadowy form of opinion is all we have. Were Protagoras right he might have referred to a tadpole or a pig as well as to a man for his measure. No, Plato asserts, besides opinion, whether true or false, man has also knowledge. The operation of this faculty we may not be able to analyse, but it is there, within our souls, giving us certain information of the everlasting reality of righteousness and loveliness in themselves, as things apart from the flux, and bidding us look to the God of these realities for the measure of our nature. 161c

Now, in this dualism of knowledge and opinion is found the answer to the paradoxical question as to the teachableness of virtue. Morality, as the force behind the specific virtues, is a matter of knowledge, whereas the specific virtues are dependent on what is commonly called knowledge but is really opinion; and opinion can be formed by instruction, whereas knowledge cannot be. Thus, the virtue of temperance may be described as a golden mean in our action, as a result of obedience to the precept "Nothing too much," which announces to each urgent desire: So far shalt thou go and no further. If, for example, we eat a certain amount and kind of food (and no chance intervene), we shall be healthy and enjoy the pleasure of health; if we transgress through ignorance or wilfulness, we shall surely injure our health and suffer the pains of disease. And so it is with all the other activities of life, under whichever of the specific virtues they may fall. Our judgement of the point at which any activity ceases to be a virtue and becomes a vice is determined by a calculation of consequences in pleasure and pain, and the rightness or wrongness of our calculation will depend on our own experience and on the similar experience of others. The experience of others is imparted to us by instruction, and so it is that the specific virtues are teachable; we can go to a man of experience to learn the nature of temperance and bravery and wisdom and justice, as we can go to a physician to learn the precepts of his art.

Hence the weight which Plato lays on the education of youth in the choice and control of pleasures and pains. In the average and in the long run the man so trained, having the tradition of society to correct his own narrower experience, will act instinctively on a proper calculation. But it is to be noted that this trained instinct, though the only guide we have in our specific acts, casts no more than a flickering light. Thus, bravery, when it rises to the dignity of a virtue, is determined by a man's opinion of what should be feared and what should not, and of the extent to which he should give rein to his impulses of hostility and self-defence. It is a reckoning of the balance of pleasure consequent upon his own safety and upon the rewards of public esteem. But our judgement can never be infallible in such matters: any man, by an error of calculation, may attack where true bravery would have counselled retreat, or may retreat where true bravery would have counselled attack. The outcome, moreover, is subject to hazards beyond the scope of his consideration. In an attack which from the point of view of his company is prudent, he may be the one who falls into the hands of the enemy; and he may suffer torture and death in such a way that his act of true courage may end, so far as he personally is concerned, in pain, and no pleasure at all. At the best, though we have an immediate intuition of pleasure and pain as present realities, as soon as we begin to calculate consequences in order to act, our judgement can be verified only *ex post facto,* and the virtues cannot be raised out of the region of uncertain opinion.

This treachery of calculation is what tends to drag the hedonist down to the sty, bidding him distrust the more elusive rewards of virtue and lay hold of any pleasure near at hand whose punishment is not swift and visible. If there be any steady law of conduct it must be referred to a principle freed from the chances of fortune and so fortified against the immediate cravings of appetite. For this principle, as we have seen, Plato turned to the moral impulsion behind the specific virtues. In the *Laws* he identified it with wisdom, but with a wisdom drawn from the soul's knowledge of herself as divine and akin to God, a wisdom quite different from the virtue identical with a calculating prudence. In *The Republic* the same moral impulsion was called justice; but there again justice was so defined as to be synonymous with a form of knowledge; it was the intuition commanded in the Delphic salutation "Know thyself," as the virtues are taught in the other Delphic precept, "Nothing too much." And this higher knowledge, as we have also seen, is not vague or empty of content, but rich with fruition. It, too, is concerned with a state of feeling—not those pleasures, in which the opinions of virtue have their range, but the happiness present in the soul with the purpose to act virtuously and dependent on that purpose alone. No man can impart this knowledge to us, though he may exhort us to look more intently into the nature of our being; the knowledge of the happiness of morality is not teachable, but comes to each of us secretly, by what Plato, speaking mythologically, calls a "divine chance."

I would not for a moment maintain that no difficulties adhere to this dualism, partly implicit and partly explicit in the philosophy of Plato, which sets pleasure, virtue, and opinion in one group, and over against them happiness, morality, and knowledge. We are here, let us admit frankly, in the region of paradox. Indeed dualism is but another name for that Socratic Paradox which results from accepting simultaneously both the spiritual affirmation of Socrates and his identification of virtue with knowledge, (that is, with opinion, as something distinct from the knowledge of the spirit). It is of the nature of the dualistic intuition that it cannot be ultimately explained by reason, but we can perhaps make its operation clearer by an illustration.

When Socrates lay in prison, awaiting the day of execution, he was visited by one of his powerful friends, Crito, who pressed money upon him to bribe his way out and so to escape an unfair doom. Socrates' reply is given in the Dialogue that goes by the name of his friend. The conversation turns on two main theses. First Socrates asks Crito whether he still abides by their old decision of former days, that it is better, no matter what the circumstances may be, to do justice than to do injustice, better to suffer injustice patiently, if needs be, than to do wrong in return. To this thesis Crito is committed, and he will not now draw back. And note that there is no real discussion here, but a direct appeal to the moral intuition; for, as Socrates declares, between one who assents to this affirmation of the spirit and one who dissents there is no common ground of debate, but each necessarily will look with contempt on the views of the other. Then follows the question: What is the right course of conduct for me, Socrates, under the particular circumstances in which I am now placed? How shall I do justice? This is not a matter of intuition, to be settled by an affirmation, but a point to be argued out and decided on its merits, like any other specific case of virtue. And what is the argument? In the first place Socrates repeats the statement of the *Apology,* that we have no certain knowledge of death whether it be a good thing for man or an evil thing. So far the principle of scepticism rules. But men have learned by experience that it is a good thing for a city to be governed by laws; since then only is order possible, and that like-mindedness of citizens on which hang all the strength and blessings of civilization. By our very birth and education and voluntary residence in a city we have entered into a kind of contract with it, and we ought either to submit to the laws as they are or to bring about the passage of other laws. That is what men mean by justice, that we should obey the behests of the city or persuade it to think otherwise; and, in view of our ignorance of death and money and so many other things of the sort that seem to people to affect their personal welfare, the pursuit of justice is probably the best calculation of pleasures a man can make. Moreover, by obedience to the laws of men we shall put ourselves into harmony with the spirit of law in general, and with the peaceful and orderly movement of the universe. Therefore, Socrates reasons, it is better for me to stay here where I am, and to abide by the voice of the laws of Athens.

Now, in this discussion of law and duty Socrates says not a word which would not have been accepted by John Stuart Mill. Wherein, then, is the difference between Socrates' position and that of a high-minded utilitarian? When it comes to the decision of a particular case, they argue and decide alike; both reach the same definition of what is just, and both say that this decision must be followed at the risk of losing money and comfort and even life itself. So far they agree, but at this point they part company, and their ways are in opposite directions. To Mill there was nothing beyond the decision, nothing (in his philosophy taken literally, that is, for in his character he was inconsistent) to give validity to the decision of virtue when it might be weakened by doubts. For, after all, any such calculation as this made by

Socrates, and as would be made by Mill, is in the region of guessing; unless it can be reinforced by some surer intuition, it will yield to men in general only a treacherous foundation for conduct, and this enforcing power of intuition is precisely what Socrates had and what utilitarianism lacks. Suppose there was an error in the reasoning of Socrates when he refused the opportunity, as Crito says, not only to carry on a life of virtue but to provide for the proper training of his children—suppose Crito was right and Socrates was wrong (as the case might well be), what recompense was there for a man who sacrificed himself for an empty name? And without the assurance of some criterion other than the very fallible calculations of reason and the conflicting precepts of tradition, from what source was a man in Socrates' position to draw the strength of character that should withstand the temptations of the nearer pleasure? There is no such resource in the philosophy of hedonism. But Socrates did not waver. He *knew* that it was better to do justice than to do injustice, not because justice would probably bring to him the larger pleasure as a man living in a city and universe of law (though this too he guessed), but because the very intention of doing justice certainly brought its sufficient reward. The feeling of happiness associated with moral purpose was so much more real to him than were the stings of pleasure and pain that, under its compulsion, he could afford to laugh at the doubts which might weaken his loyalty to apparent virtue by contrasting the security of immediate pleasure with the insecurity of a long calculation, and by pitting the intensity of personal desires against the duller sense of participating in the public good.

Fortunately for the world the common sense of mankind is more in conformity with a hedonism complemented, as it was in Socrates, by intuition and scepticism, than with a hedonism that thinks it unnecessary to look for any guide beyond the light of its own tremulous lamp.

CHAPTER V

PSYCHOLOGY

PLATO'S ethical philosophy is connected, as any system of ethics must be connected, with a particular way of regarding the soul. Its end is in psychology, and we are thus brought face to face with a problem of consistency: the soul under his analysis fell into three faculties (if we may use this word without its modern psychological implications), yet his ethics is essentially dualistic. How are these two positions to be reconciled?

The apparent discrepancy of Plato's philosophy in this matter has troubled more than one of the commentators on *The Republic.* In a note on a 602c critical passage of the tenth book James Adam has these significant words:

"The reasoning from here to 607A has been supposed to rest on a psychological theory irreconcilable with that of Book iv, to which the discussion expressly alludes (in 602E). See for example Krohn *Pl. St.* p. 255 and Pfleiderer *Zur Lösung* etc. p. 38. It is true that Plato is here content, in view of his immediate purpose, with a twofold division of the soul into (1) a rational and (2) an irrational, *alogiston* (604D, 605B), or lower element. But the resemblance between the two theories is greater than the difference, for (a) the *logistikon* is common to both, and (b) on its moral side the irrational element appears sometimes as the *epithymêtikon* (606D), sometimes as a degenerate form of the *thymoeides* (604E, 606A)."

The point is well taken, and is enforced chiefly by the characterization of the good man under the stress of adversity. "There is," says Plato, "a principle of reason and law in him which commands him to resist, and there is likewise the sense of his misfortune which is forcing him to indulge his sorrow. But when a man is drawn in contrary directions at once in regard to the same object, we say that there must be two elements in him. The law affirms that to be patient under suffering is best, and that we should not give way to impatience, since in fact it is not clear whether our state is good or evil, and anyhow nothing is gained by resentment; none of the events of human life is of serious importance, and grief stands in the way of that state which we need to attain as speedily as possible. Then there is the other principle, which inclines us to recollection of our troubles and to lamentations, and can never have enough of them; this we may call irrational, futile, and

604A

cowardly." Such a description admits of no ambiguity. On one side it sets the governing, controlling, inhibiting energy of the soul, working to the end of law and reason; on the other side, all that part of the soul which suffers and desires and which is repugnant to self-mastery. Mr. Adam was correct in arguing that this analysis is only superficially inconsistent with the psychology of the fourth book, but he errs, I think, in holding that the dualism here imposed on the threefold division of the faculties is for immediate purposes alone, rather than fundamental to Plato's philosophy. He might have been warned of this error by a consideration of the series of portraits of the eighth and ninth books, from which was drawn the account of the Tyrant's Progress, and which is avowedly a return to the interrupted argument of the fourth book.

What is the cause of that degeneration from the highest type of liberty down to the basest condition of slavery? The just and good man is called the aristocrat for the reason that he is governed by the moral force which is the better of the two halves of his nature. When the worse half breaks from this control and begins to act for itself, the balance of the soul is disturbed; but the rebellious desires are still at first of a specious kind, the ambitions of elevated rank and authority which have very much the look of pure virtues. The next step is taken when the weight of desire passes to a lower form of ambition, and the man begins to crave money as the material reality beneath everything the world reverences. For a while the spendthrift passions are held in subjection by a kind of mild compulsion. But this balance is precarious; the desire for money, following the nature of any desire, grows more and more excessive, until the very excess leads to a revolt of the other desires. Then we see the emergence of the distracted soul, across which all desires move with equal authority and to which all passions are in turn equally alluring. Again the change comes from the tendency to unbridled expansion which is in the very nature of desire. Soon there is a contention among all the loosened passions, until some one evil and devouring lust gathers strength above its rivals, and snatches a despotism, the last and most miserable state of a man's soul.

Certainly if anything is evident throughout the whole course of this decline, it is that the soul is regarded as composed of two warring elements, and that the descending steps are measured by the degree to which one of these elements throws off obedience to the other. The sum of the matter is in the words of the *Laws:* "To have won the victory over pleasures, this is to live happily, the

850c

life of felicity, but to fail before them is the very opposite." This does not mean, as the preceding discussion of the *Laws* abundantly proves, that pleasure is in itself a thing to be scorned, or is in its nature necessarily destructive of happiness; but it does mean that pleasure may on occasion draw us away from our true goal, and that happiness is dependent on the dominance of one member of the soul over the other.

The dualism of Plato's psychology is less entangled in other Dialogues where the classification of the virtues does not come so prominently into view as in *The Republic*. Thus, in the *Phaedo*, it falls into rather a harsh opposition between the soul and the body (*sôma* = *sêma*), and in this form, unfortunately, it was to be taken up by the Christian Platonists and developed into an asceticism which, with Plato, had been only a passing phase of philosophic bitterness. It is to be remembered, also, that even in the *Phaedo* the "body" is really not so much the material flesh as a symbol for all that part of the soul which is swayed by the baser desires. For, as it is argued in the first *Alcibiades*, a man is a different thing from the body which he uses, neither is he both body and soul, but soul; and in the tenth book of *The Republic*, where Plato is arguing for immortality, he traces the source of evil to the soul itself, as

129E ff

distinct from the body, with no uncertain note. So strong is this thought of the inner dualism that in his later years he would even speak as if we were not one soul but two. In this way his dualism colours the mythology of the *Timaeus:*

"He himself [God] was creator of the divine, but the creation of the mortal he laid upon his offspring to accomplish. And they, in imitation of his act, took from him the immortal element of soul, and then fashioned about her a mortal body, and gave her all the body as a vehicle; and in it they framed also another kind of soul, which is mortal, having in itself dreadful and compelling passions—pleasure first, the greatest incitement to evil, then pains that frighten away good, and besides these confidence and fear, witless counsellors both, and wrath hard to appease, and alluring hope. Having mingled these with irrational sensation and with love that stops at nothing, they composed as they could the mortal soul of man." 69c

In the *Laws,* by a change of allegory, the soul is regarded as herself the creator, instead of the created, and as such the source of all good and evil in the world, of what is beautiful and what is ugly, just and unjust. From her proceed the passions and powers of man, and from her proceed the motions that rule the heavens and every moving creature—yet not from one soul but from 896c ff two souls, the beneficent and the worker of all that is contrary.

In view of this persistent dualism it is clear that the three faculties of Plato's psychology are not independently co-operative powers, but merely different phases, sometimes sharply dissociated, sometimes merging into one another, of the activity of what we may call, using a terminology strange to Plato, the personal element of our being. The faculties might have been four or five or any other number, instead of three, if the analysis of the virtues had been carried further—if, for instance, bravery had been subdivided into endurance and aggressiveness. The only obscurity in this scheme is chargeable to Plato's careless treatment of the word "reason" when he passes from epistemology to ethics. By employing the same term now for the higher of the two elements of the soul, and now for the prudential faculty of the lower element, he introduced, or at least encouraged, an ambiguity which has never to this day been purged from the body of philosophy, as any one may know who will trace the meaning of "reason" and "rational" through the seventeenth and eighteenth centuries down into modern literature. In one place you will find Plato drawing the reason close to the desires, as in the passage of *The Republic* which deals with

411c ff

education under the two heads of "music" (including literature, etc.) and gymnastic. Here reason and the concupiscent faculty, taken together as opposed to the *thymoeides,* have their discipline in music, whereas the *thymoeides* is fortified by gymnastic. Yet in another part of the same Dialogue the *thymoeides* is regarded as the spirit of indignation and self-respect which is normally on the side of judgement against the desires. In either case the assimilation of the reason whether to the desires or to the *thymoeides* shows that we have to do here with a prudential faculty different in kind from reason regarded as an element of the soul set over against all the practical activities.

439E ff

A hint of this double nature of reason may be found in the most picturesque presentation of Plato's psychology—the famous metaphor of the chariot in the *Phaedrus.* Superficially, the division is tripartite, as made by the driver, representing reason, and his two horses, the one docile, the other self-willed; but, more carefully considered, the image shows the usual dualism under a novel guise. When the soul comes into sight of a fair and beloved object, the wild horse rushes forward to satisfy his base lust, dragging along with him his mate (the *thymoeides,* as instinctive self-respect) and the driver. At first the driver and the better horse resist ineffectually; but of a sud-

246A ff

den there comes to the driver a remembrance of the pure external beauty he has beheld in a previous existence with the gods, and, as it were, smitten by that vision, he himself is thrown backwards and pulls both the horses to their haunches. By this check the driver and the docile horse gain control of the concupiscent beast, and the soul is turned from its evil deed. The power of resistance came at last, not from the driver as a deliberative agent, but from the knowledge that belongs to a diviner reason, and strikes into him after the manner of the Christian's grace of God.[1]

Republic 439E

But Plato's symbolism is interpreted more clearly by the story of a certain Leontius, who, coming up to the city one day by the north wall, was troubled by the sight of some dead bodies lying in the place of execution. For a while he was divided between his curiosity and a feeling of repulsion, and stood with closed eyes, debating with himself. But at last his desire got the mastery, and, forcing open his eyes, he ran up to the place, crying, "Look, ye wretches, take your fill of the lovely spectacle!" The moral of the tale, Plato adds, is the distinction between the *thymoeides* and the desires, as proved by their enmity. But it suggests something more than that. The

[1] So Chrysostom, *In Eph.* 36E, sets the spirit above the driver, as the driver is set above the horses. See also Greg. Naz. III, 1382 (Migne).

deliberative pause of Leontius, while reason and self-respect are contending with desire, points to the function of that element of the soul, whether it be called reason or by another name, which is above them all, and upon whose exercise rests the possibility of forming judgements and determining our actions.[2] The problem of Platonic psychology is to define, or at least to understand as clearly as may be possible, the operation of this dualism. In a general way the substratum of the lower element of the soul is easily found in the desires and emotions (the *thymoeides* is, succinctly, the desires as these assume the guise of personal emotions); the difficulty is in coming to terms with the higher element.

It is tempting to associate this governing principle with the free will, or *liberum arbitrium,* which has been a theme of metaphysical debate ever since it was brought into prominence by the contest of the orthodox Church with the Pelag-

[2] Schleiermacher, in his note to *Republic* 572A, gives a clear statement of this separate governing element of the soul: "Ich will aber hier, wenn auch nur im Vorbeigehen, aufmerksam darauf machen, wie ausser den dreien, dem begehrlichen, dem eifrigen und dem vernünftigen, noch ein vierter, nämlich der von jenen dreien bald dieses bald jenes beschwichtigende oder aufregende sich einschleicht; so dass nun dieser hier der Fuhrmann wird, und wir ein Dreigespann haben nebst einem Fuhrmann, wie es scheint, indem was im Phaidros der Fuhrmann war, hier als Ross erscheint, und zwar nicht in einer in gleichem Grade bildlichen Darstellung."—This is good Platonism, except that Schleiermacher's *aufregende,* though a literal translation of Plato's *κινήσας*, shows, as I hope to prove, a mistaken notion of the action of the governing faculty.

ians; and there is, perhaps, no better way to obtain a clear notion of the intention of Plato's psychology than by turning aside for a moment to the last great discussion of this question in modern times. For the support of the Calvinistic doctrine of predestination against the Pelagian error of the Arminians, Jonathan Edwards had, in his *Treatise Concerning Human Affections*, denied the existence of any such faculty as the will in the ordinary sense of the word. The will, or the heart as he calls it, is merely the inclination of the soul towards the good as this is present to us at the moment of action. This thesis was later taken up and developed in his inquiry into the *Freedom of the Will*. Here, to clinch his argument for the identity of will and inclination, he uses the illustration of a drunkard who has liquor before him and must choose whether to drink or not; and he proves that the so-called volition of the drunkard will certainly be in accord with "what, in the present view of his mind, taken in the whole of it, is most agreeable to him." That is well; and so far Plato would assent, for there is no place in his psychology, any more than in the theology of Calvin, for a positive faculty of the will as a force independent of our inclination. But Edwards failed to discriminate sufficiently between two classes of motives impelling a man to action: the immediate physical craving and the memory of pains and pleasures stored up in the mind by experience. Now, these latter are more sluggish in operation than the former; they are at a disadvantage, so to speak, unless the physical desire is held in check until they acquire a kind of cumulative weight. The liberty of the soul might thus appear to reside, not in the determination of a positive will—which must indeed obey the strongest motive at the moment of action—but in the power of holding all motives in suspense until a due balance has been struck.

In fact the theory did come to Edwards in just this form, and in two sections of his Inquiry he makes a diversion from his main argument to consider it. The actual treatise against which he directs his contentions, though he does not name it, was undoubtedly Isaac Watts's *Essay on the Freedom of Will in God and the Creature;* but the theory itself has stronger authorities behind it than this mild Arminian, and needs to be considered historically. Its lineage goes back to Descartes.

The Cartesian philosophy made no generic distinction between the will and the understanding; it regarded the will as the act of selection among the various data of the senses, by which act we form the ideas in the understanding. The sensations themselves are not deceptive, and if we fall into error, it is because the will draws inferences and makes inadequate judgements. Truth is measured by the clearness of our ideas, and right action is dependent on the truth of the ideas behind it.

Malebranche also taught that we act in accordance with our inclinations and that our inclinations are the result of our judgements; but he goes beyond Descartes in his ethical deductions. Error, he thinks, is due to the inherent restlessness of the human will, which is drawn to the multiplicity and vanity of sensible objects, and so fails to make true judgements of the value of things. Hence the process of attaining a true judgement is by an act of attention on the part of the mind;[3] and hence, also, the general law of truth and conduct: "We should never give our entire assent except to propositions which appear so evidently true that we cannot reject them without feeling an inner pain and the secret reproach of reason; that is to say, without knowing clearly that our unwillingness to assent would be an abuse of our liberty."[4]

The idealism of Malebranche, variously modified in the transit, was brought into England by John Norris, who, though himself an Oxonian,

[3] *Recherche de la Vérité*, Préface.
[4] *Ibid.* I, ii, 4; repeated, VI, i.

forms an interesting link between the Cambridge Platonists of the seventeenth century and the deistic writers of the eighteenth. He takes, for our purpose, an important step forwards by associating Malebranche's "act of attention" explicitly with the problem of the freedom of the will.[5] The place of Norris in English philosophy has received such scant consideration that it may be worth while to quote from him at some length on this point:

"In the first place 'tis agreed betwixt us that there must be a *to eph' hêmin,* some principle of free agency in man. All that does or can fall under debate is what is the primary and immediate subject of this free agency. Now this, being a rational perfection, must be primarily subjected either in the understanding or in the will, or, to speak more accurately, either in the soul as intelligent or in the soul as volent. That the latter cannot be the root of liberty will be sufficiently clear if this one proposition be fully made out, viz., that the will necessarily follows the dictate of the understanding, or that the soul necessarily wills as she understands.

"Now for the demonstration of this, I shall

[5] The connexion between attention and liberty is, no doubt, implicit in Malebranche. Thus he says (I, i, 2) that liberty consists in the "ability to suspend one's judgement and one's love," and "to make our natural inclinations terminate in some particular object." But I do not remember that he has brought this notion of attention and liberty to bear clearly on the problem of the freedom of the will, and passages of the sixth book place the act of attention itself in a secondary, or at least an ambiguous, position.

desire but this one *postulatum,* which I think all the schools of learning will allow me, viz., that the object of the soul as volent is apparent good, or that the soul cannot will evil as evil. Now good apparent, or evil apparent, is the same in other terms with that which is apprehended or judged to be good or evil respectively. . . . If, therefore, good apparent be the object of the will, good apprehended will be so too, and consequently the soul necessarily wills as she understands; otherwise she will choose evil as evil, which is against the supposition. . . .

"The soul, therefore, as volent cannot be the immediate subject of liberty. If, therefore, there be any such thing as free agency, the seat of it must be in the soul as intelligent. But, does not the soul necessarily understand as the object appears, as well as she necessarily wills as she understands? She does so, and therefore I do not place the seat of liberty in the soul as judging, or forming a judgement, for that I confess to be determined by the appearance of things. But, though it be necessary that the soul judge as things appear, yet 'tis not necessary (except only in self-evident propositions) that things should appear thus or thus, but that will wholly depend upon the degrees of advertency, or attention; such a degree being requisite to make the object appear thus, and such a degree to appear otherwise. And this advertency is that wherein I place the seat of free agency. Lower than this I discern not the least glimpse of it, and higher I cannot go. Here, therefore, I conceive I have good reason to fix, and to affirm that the only *autexousion* of the soul consists in her having an immediate power to attend or not attend, or to attend more or less. I say an *immediate* power; for if you will have an express act of the will interposed, that act of the will must have a practical judgement, that judgement an objective appearance, that appearance another attention, that attention another will, and so on *ad infinitum*. I think it therefore reasonable to stop at the first."

These passages occur in Norris's reply (undated) to a letter of Henry More's dated January 16, 1685/6, but the correspondence was not printed until 1688, when it formed a supplement to Norris's *Theory and Regulation of Love*.[6] Locke's *Essay* appeared two years after the publication of this correspondence, and it is a nice question to guess whether he had felt the influence of Norris's theory. The writer of the letter he afterwards characterized as "an obscure enthusiastic gentleman," nor was Locke himself at all of the school of Malebranche; yet one of the most striking chapters of the *Essay* (I, xxi) is substantially a development of the Norrisian conception of free will and attention.

Locke starts with a thoroughly hedonistic conception of life. That which is properly good or

6 I quote from the second edition, 1694.

bad, he says, is nothing but barely pleasure or pain, the distinction, of course, being carried into the distant consequences of our acts. Happiness is not different in kind from pleasure, but is merely the utmost pleasure we are capable of, and misery the utmost pain. All men naturally desire happiness, and would always act with this end in view, were will and desire the same thing. But the will is perfectly distinguished from desire; it is determined not by what we desire, that is happiness, but by the most important and urgent uneasiness we at any time feel. And this follows from the nature of our happiness and misery. All present pain, whatever it be, makes a part of our present misery; but all absent good does not at any time make a necessary part of our present happiness, nor does the absence of it make a part of our misery. On the other hand change itself is attended with some uneasiness; so that, unless the absence of good in some way is made present to us by a feeling of uneasiness, it does not move us to change our conduct. Thus, all men desire happiness, but when they are rid of pain they are apt to take up with the pleasure at hand.

Wherein then does liberty consist? It is not in desire, for the desire of happiness is a necessity of our nature. Nor is it, properly speaking, in the will; for freedom of the will is merely an external consideration, being the absence of any restraint preventing us from acting in accordance with the impulsion of present uneasiness. The place of liberty is in the mind, or, following Locke's own terminology, it is and it is not in the will. As a matter of fact the *Essay* here admits into the discussion a confusion of terms of which Edwards was not slow to take advantage. In one place Locke says that the "power which the mind has thus to order the consideration of any idea, or the forbearing to consider it, . . . is that which we call the will"; but elsewhere he takes the position, more consistent with his general system, that a man is "determined in willing by his own thought and judgement what is best for him to do." The will is evidently taken in two ways, first as a power of directing our thought, which is a matter of internal liberty; and secondly as a power of acting in accordance with our thought, which is an internal necessity and a matter of external liberty conditioned by circumstances. The power of directing our thought should in fact not have been called the will at all (unless, at least, it was distinguished, by some such phrase as the *will to refrain,* from the positive will as ordinarily conceived); nor is it rightly identified with the mind, but is above the mind and purely negative in character.

Now it may sound strange to use the attribute "negative of that higher power in which our liberty resides." It is so termed because, as Locke himself says, it is the power within the mind to *suspend* the execution and satisfaction of any of its desires, and the consequent liberty to consider the objects of all the desires and weigh them one against the other. "In this," he continues, "lies the liberty man has; and from the not using of it right comes all that variety of mistakes, errors, and faults which we run into in the conduct of our lives, and our endeavours after happiness; whilst we precipitate the determination of our wills, and engage too soon before due examination. To prevent this, we have a power to suspend the prosecution of this or that desire, as every one daily may experiment in himself. This seems to me the source of all liberty; in this seems to consist that which is (as I think improperly) called free-will. For during this suspension of any desire, before the will be determined to action, and the action (which follows that determination) done, we have opportunity to examine, view and judge of the good or evil of what we are going to do; and when, upon due examination, we have judged, we have done our duty, all that we can or ought to do in pursuit of our happiness; and it is not a fault, but a perfection of our nature, to desire, will, and act according to the last result of a fair examination."

Locke's view of liberty, then, is essentially the same as Norris's: liberty is the power of attention, by which we may bring the ideas of absent good and future pleasure and of evil and pain into the mind in such a way that they may compete with the pressure of immediate pleasure or uneasiness. It is, to go back to Descartes, the power to form clear and adequate judgements. But by regarding this power *negatively*, as a mere act of suspension, Locke has given it a profounder and truer psychological standing as an element of the soul apart from that other element which reasons and remembers and desires. He makes it the inhibiting check by virtue of which reason and memory and desire are enabled to arrive at a proper balance and to result in right conduct. Locke, however, did not perceive, or perceiving shirked, the radical conclusions that ought to follow his theory. Otherwise he would not have clung to the hedonism which regards happiness as nothing more than the sum of pleasure, but would have distinguished generically between happiness and pleasure, attributing happiness to that element of our being which gives us the power of suspension, and leaving pleasure to the consequences of our particular course of action. Some inkling of this distinction he seems to have had when to the ordinary balance of calculable pleasures and pains he added the hope and fear of eternal happiness or misery in another life. "But when," he says, "infinite happiness is put into one scale, against infinite misery in the other, if the worst that comes to the pious man, if he mistakes, be the best that the wicked man can attain to if he be in the right, who can without madness run into the venture?" Heaven and hell, as the reward attached to the moral state of the soul rather than to the particular virtue or vice of our conduct, are, in fact, the mythological equivalent for Plato's philosophical distinction between happiness and pleasure, misery and pain. But from the attainment of this deeper insight Locke was prevented by the whole weight of his sensational system.

Locke's presentation of the problem of freedom came to Edwards apparently, as I have said, through the mediation of Watts. With the contentions of the ordinary Arminians, who insisted on a separation between will and inclination and sought for the source of evil in a voluntary choice of action contrary to known good and happiness, the Puritan divine had an easy task; and from this point of view his argument against free-will ("improperly" so-called, as Locke declared) has never been answered. But with the theory as developed by Descartes, Malebranche, Norris, and

Locke his path was not so smooth. Twice, as I have said, he undertook to reply to Watts, without naming him, and once he struck at the heart of the question, declaring that "this suspension of volition, if there be properly any such thing, is itself an act of volition"—with the obvious conclusions. To this objection Norris had already replied; but our Arminian might have argued further that the act of suspension, or will to refrain, really implies an essentially different order of choice from that of the positive will, or inclination. Two desires are not set before it to choose between, but the purpose to be self-determined or not, the intention to be in a state to choose wisely or not; the actual choice of one course of action or another must come after the suspension is made, and is the work of the imagination and the discursive reason balanced against a present desire. Returning again to the question whether our freedom depends on an act of suspension apart from the positive will, Edwards endeavours to evade it by pointing to its moral implication. "If," he says, "determining thus to suspend and consider be that act of the will wherein alone liberty is exercised, then in this all virtue and vice must consist. . . . According to such a supposition the most horrid crimes, adultery, murder, sodomy, blasphemy, &c., do not at all consist in the horrid nature of the things themselves, but only in the neglect of thorough consideration before they were perpetrated, which brings their viciousness to a small matter and makes all crimes equal." To which the Arminian might have retorted by distinguishing between the moral state of the agent, which depends on the degree of his self-control, and the virtue or vice of any particular act, which depends on the pleasure or pain ultimately resulting from the act.

Now, however Plato's psychological terminology may vary from Dialogue to Dialogue, or from page to page, there is always in the background of his ethics this notion of the governing element of the soul as an absolute inhibition, or power of suspension. And despite the differences of time and circumstance, his path to this position was very much like that traversed by the French and English philosophers. We can see this in his recourse to the same illustration as that afterwards employed by Locke and Edwards. In *The Republic* he analyses the state of a man who feels a desire to drink but is restrained by thought of the remoter consequences. At first reading, the reason, as the restraining faculty, might seem to be merely one impulse (*to kôluon*) opposing another impulse (*to keleuon*); but look more attentively and you will detect here, in the usual

473B ff

double twist of the word "reason" when applied by Plato to ethical matters, precisely the Lockian point of view against which the Edwardsian argument for predestination finally broke. Reason, on the one hand, is a realizing sense of the future as contrasted with the present craving, but it is also something above both these contending inclinations, a something which forbids one of them from encroaching on the province of the other, and by holding them in leash makes possible a proper balance and control. This conception of the higher reason is, it must be admitted, rather latent than explicit in these passages of *The Republic,* but no room is left for doubting Plato's meaning if we take into account his development of the Socratic self-knowledge on its sceptical side as an inhibition upon the presumption of knowledge in the ordinary sense of the word. "To seem to know," says Plato in the *Sophist,* "when we do not know, is the source of those errors in judgement to which we are all prone"; and further, in the first *Alcibiades:*[7] "Through this same ignorance, which leads us to think we know when we do not know, come our errors of practice." That is Plato's way of expressing Malebranche's first law of judgement

229C

117D

[7] Whether genuine or not, I have not scrupled to use this and other passages of the first *Alcibiades* as thoroughly Platonic in conception. They could be abundantly confirmed from the Dialogues of unquestioned authenticity.

and conduct and Locke's theory of suspension. And Plato owes his supremacy in the world of thought to the consistency of his insight where his great successors drew back in a kind of metaphysical alarm. The Lockian position presupposes a radical dualism, and has no real validity against predestinarianism, or any other form of determinism, unless this foundation is accepted, with all its consequences. It was because Locke, led astray by his sensational philosophy, failed to develop this truth that his theory of freedom misses logical finality and has been forgotten or rejected by most modern psychologists. In like manner Malebranche, though he took the opposite direction from Locke's, lost his splendid opportunity because, in his effort to escape the mechanical dualism of Descartes, he fell into the abyss of pantheism. It was just here that Plato showed the depth and courage of his conviction, by the thoroughgoing dualism of his philosophy. He was mainly, I think, kept in the strait and narrow path by fidelity to his master; and to understand the nature of that element of the soul in which he placed human freedom and morality, we have yet to see how it is related to the most singular, and to some persons the most puzzling, aspect of Socrates' religious conviction.

There is a beautiful passage in the fourth book

of the *Memorabilia* which rises in tone above the usual wont of Xenophon, as if he were here writing of things he but half comprehended. Socrates has been expounding the many gracious bounties bestowed by the gods upon mankind, and concludes with the supreme gift of reason and discourse by which men are distinguished from animals. "And more," he adds, "when we are unable to foresee what is advantageous for us in the future, the gods are still with us, telling us, if we consult them, of things to come by the voice of prophecy, and teaching us what is best." "But with you, Socrates," his interlocutor replies, "they seem to deal more kindly than with other men, since even without your asking they forewarn you of what should be done and what not." And Socrates acknowledges the truth of this favour, but declares that another man may attain to the same harmony with the divine, "if he will not wait to see the gods in their actual forms, but will be content, discerning their works, to honour and worship them." "For consider but the soul of man," he continues, "which, if it can be said of anything human, partakes of the divine; manifestly it rules in us as a king, yet is not seen at all. Whence we should learn not to despise things invisible, but from their acts should infer their power, and so do honour to the divine immanence [*to daimonion*]."

This reverential regard for the daemonic guidance was, in fact, the religion of Socrates. One of the clauses of the indictment against him, it will be remembered, was that he denied the gods of the city, and introduced strange daemonic powers of his own. To this charge Xenophon replied by a flat contradiction, averring that Socrates not only himself observed carefully the official worship but taught others to look for the will of the gods in what we should now term the State religion. Plato took a double course with the accusation. First he leads the plaintiff in the trial to widen the charge so as to embrace pure atheism, and then pounces on the absurdity of indicting the same man for denying the existence of gods and for introducing new gods. Secondly, he brings into view the innocence and genuine piety of the Socratic faith. Now the truth of the matter would seem to be this: though there is every reason to believe that Socrates, like Plato after him, conformed in the main to the common religious practices of the day, being too sincerely sceptical to set up the dictates of private doubt against the intuition that might lie half-concealed in the popular myths, yet he was in the deepest sense of the word an innovator. However clumsily his accusers may have formulated their indictment, and whatever political aim they may have had in view, they were right in seeing this. The daemonic voice, or divine immanence, to which Socrates yielded perfect obedience, may not have been a strange god added to the pantheon, as his enemies asserted, but it did bring a new and strange faith into Athens and the world, the faith of philosophy.[8]

Republic 496c

Many men since that day have asked themselves what this portent might be; some have wondered reverentially, and some have scoffed at Socrates as an ordinary dupe of fanaticism if not the victim of an epileptic delusion. Plato, apparently having no direct cue from his master, interpreted the phenomenon in various ways. At one time he speaks of the daemon, or, more vaguely, the daemonic, as if it were merely the spark of divine intelligence implanted by God in every soul. Again it might be an exclusive gift to Socrates and, possibly, to some few others. Besides its looser kinship with the divine, it might appear as Socrates' "guardian, a very god," or, more bravely, as "God." At other times the mythological symbolism, if we may so call it, falls away, and leaves the naked spirit of the man, as it were the higher self speaking to the lower. So when Socrates con-

[8] Justin Martyr (*Apol.* I, v, 3) saw clearly that in this respect Socrates was in the same position as the Christians.

Hippias Major 304B 298B

trasts his own hesitating ways with the magnificent assurance of one of the sophists, he ascribes the cause of his embarrassment to some daemonic chance, or fortune, that has taken possession of him. If he heeds the bidding of this power and refrains from everything but the search for truth, then the mighty men of the tongue deride his incompetence; and if he hearkens to them and regards truth as a minor matter in comparison with success, then he must listen to all sorts of reproaches from a man who is always standing by to expose him. This fellow, he says, is closely related to him and lives in the same house with him; and when he goes home, scolds him in private. And who is this troublesome spy whom nothing can escape? Why, it is just Socrates, the son of Sophroniscus!

All this is very tantalizing for those scholars who must put a ticket and a name on everything. But one fact is certain: whether it be a god, or very God, or the man's self, or some less definable intimation of the divine will, the daemonic guide invariably takes the form of an inhibition, and never of a positive command. On this one point Plato, whom we may trust in such a matter above Xenophon, leaves us in no doubt whatever: "From childhood it has been with me," Plato makes Socrates say in the *Apology,* "as it were a

31D

voice speaking at intervals, always warning me against something I had in mind to do, never urging me to act." It was this inhibitive aspect of the Socratic religion which Plato never forgot, and which justifies us in connecting the daemonic admonition symbolically with the principle of liberty and morality in the Platonic psychology. There is a phrase in the first Dialogue with Alcibiades, whether Plato's or some good Platonist's, which I have always cherished as a peculiarly happy attempt to name the unnamable. Socrates is explaining to the petulant youth why for so many years, while other admirers were paying assiduous court, he alone has refrained until now. "The cause," Socrates replies, "was nothing human, but some daemonic check (*daimonion enantiôma*)." The incident is trivial; but in these words I seem to see the Socratic religion and the Platonic philosophy bound together by an indissoluble bond. We may not know what this *daemonic* or, as I have elsewhere translated it, this *inner check* is; we may not know why and how it acts, or why it does not act, but we do know that the clarity of our spiritual perception and the assurance of our freedom depend on keeping this will to refrain distinct from any conception of the will as a positive force.

103A

We touch here on the mystery of the spiritual

life. Men are loath to accept this purely negative view of what is highest in their being; every instinct of the concupiscent soul cries out against this complete severance between the law of the spirit and the law of nature, and the human heart revolts therefrom with all the energy and tenacity of its innate craving for flattery. Men argue in their calmer moods that such a philosophy leads nowhere save to utter abnegation of life and to a quietism that promises only the peace of death. All these arguments and repudiations I know; but, withal, I read Plato, and then read in my own soul, and the book and the voice of consciousness are one in replying that the truth of our being can be found only in the hard fact of dualism, and that the spirit, if we would define it, can be expressed only in terms of negation. Nor has this truth ever been forgotten by the world. If you turn to those Christian theologians who have most wrestled with language to give a name to their God, you will find that the attributes allowed to Him are all merely negatives of things we know by our senses.[9] And so it is in the higher schools of philosophy.

[9] "In our attempt to express what we conceive the Best of Beings and the Greatest of Felicities to be, we describe by the exact Contraries of all that we experience here—the one as *In*finite, *In*comprehensible, *Im*mutable, etc., the other as *in*corruptible, *un*defiled, and that passeth *not* away. At all events, this Coincidence, say rather Identity, of Attributes is sufficient to apprize us that to be inheritors of bliss we must become the children of God."—Bishop Leighton, quoted by Coleridge in his *Aids to Reflection*.

The Oxford idealism of T. H. Green is by no means purely Platonic, and its reduction of dualism to a relation between consciousness and nature tends to obscure the dualism within consciousness itself which is the more important aspect of the problem; yet Green's principle of consciousness is at least Platonic in this, that it can be stated only in terms of negation. "As to what that consciousness in itself or in its completeness is," he says, "we can only make negative statements. *That* there is such a consciousness is implied in the existence of the world; but *what* it is we only know through its so far acting in us as to enable us, etc."[10] It is still our fate that the command of morality is "Thou shalt not," and they who would worship God "in spirit and in truth" must worship Him as the spirit that denies, and they who would be philosophers, lovers of truth, must look to a wisdom that warns us only to abstain. He is the wise and good man who need not say, as Bolingbroke was obliged to say in an hour of remorse: "My genius, unlike the demon of Socrates, whispered so softly that very often I heard him not, in the hurry of those passions by which I was transported."

Yet it is equally true that the effects of the admonition are of the most positive sort, as can

[10] *Prolegomena* § 51.

be seen in the power and influence of the whole life of Socrates. No doubt the inhibition kept him from political activity—Jesus, too, it will be remembered, refrained from politics—but it guided him also to the noblest form of patriotism, withholding him from illegal acts at the bidding of tyrants who held life and death in their hands, and restraining him voluntarily in gaol when bribery would have opened the gates in a moment. It bade him subordinate his own welfare to those laws of the State to which he felt himself bound by a kind of tacit contract, and thus enabled him, as he thought, to bring himself into harmony with the unwritten laws of the universe of which the enacted laws of society are, as it were, the sisters. Being subject to law, he should be in unison also with the gods whose word the law is. Hence his fearlessness of death and his terrifying calmness on the field of battle. Hence the vigour of his morality, and the preservation of his chastity against such attacks of lust as are described with appalling freedom in the last scenes of the *Symposium*. Hence his resolute disregard of the conflicting opinions of men, and his loyalty to the testimony of his own soul when it prohibited the retaliation of evil for evil, though at any price of suffering and obloquy. Hence also his vocation to the life of philosophy. The same warning voice guided him in the rejection of undesirable disciples, and it was noted that those who came to him most clearly under the divine permission were speediest and surest in their spiritual growth. Through one of these disciples it made him the teacher of Greece, and the apostle to the world. The philosophy of Plato is that same voice speaking with all the splendid powers of persuasion.

Theages 129E ff

The question of the freedom of the will was forced into the domain of theology by the desire to vindicate God from the imputation of evil and to hold man accountable for his actions. And the problem of philosophic dualism goes back to the same instinctive belief in human responsibility. If a man is responsible for his acts, then he must have been free to choose between conflicting impulses; and, as we have seen, this freedom can exist only by virtue of an inhibitive power of the soul, the so-called will to refrain, entirely distinct from the positive will which is determined by the final predominance of one impulse over another. The admission of responsibility thus throws us back upon a radical psychological dualism and upon a cosmic dualism of good and evil as its counterpart. But the sense of responsibility itself springs from our immediate feelings of happiness and misery. It is of the essence of those feelings, as distinguished from pleasure and pain, that we are conscious of them as dependent upon ourselves and not upon circumstances; we are happy with the knowledge that we have chosen to act after due exercise of the inhibiting power, we are miserable with the knowledge that we have not so chosen. Thus, the consciousness of happiness and misery brings with it a sense of responsibility; the sense of responsibility leads us to a belief in the freedom of the will; the freedom of the will forces us to accept a radical dualism, psychological and cosmic. The whole argument is merely a logical evolution, so to speak, of what is implicit in the primitive fact of consciousness, since by the very consciousness of happiness and misery we are equally and immediately conscious of a radical dualism.

Now the consciousness of happiness and misery is certainly the fountain-head of Plato's ethical philosophy, and the consequent dualism of the soul is constantly present, sometimes implicit, sometimes clearly explicit, in his psychology. But it cannot be said that he followed a perfectly consistent course in regard to the other two links in the chain: the dualism of good and evil and the sense of responsibility. It remains, therefore, to examine his attitude on these two points, since the argument is so intimately concatenated that no one link can be dropped without imperilling the whole.

Plato's difficulties over the cosmic dualism of good and evil were precisely those that were later to trouble the theologians of Christianity: how shall we reconcile the presence of intrinsic evil in the world with faith in a beneficent deity? And to escape this unanswerable contradiction it must be admitted that Plato once at least fell into the fallacy so dear to Stoics and deists: God must be the cause of all things, yet God cannot be the cause of evil; hence the maladjustment and wrong we see in individual things and persons are not essentially evil, but are the mere necessity of imperfection in a world of infinite parts and pieces. The evil of the part is the good of the whole.[11]

E.g. Laws 903B

And as Plato was led at times by the paradox that confronts all theologians to remove evil somehow from the first cause, or causes, of things, and

[11] I have called this theodicy, which virtually denies the reality of evil, Stoic (cf. Marcus Aurelius ii, 3, *et passim*) and deistic (cf. Shaftesbury, *The Moralists* i, 3, *et passim*), but it is a fallacy that lies in ambush for all theology. Thomas Aquinas even introduced it into the orthodox canon of Catholicism; thus, *Summa* I, xlvii, 2: "Sicut ergo divina sapientia causa est distinctionis rerum propter perfectionem universi, ita et inaequalitatis; non enim esset perfectum universum, si tantum unus gradus bonitatis inveniretur in rebus"; and I, xlix, 3: "Puta, si quis dicat naturam ignis esse malam, quia combussit domum alicujus pauperis. Judicium autem de bonitate alicujus rei non est accipiendum secundum ordinem ad aliquid particulare, sed secundum seipsum, et secundum ordinem ad totum universum."—The same denial of the reality of evil in human sinfulness is involved in the Thomist argument in regard to primary and secondary causes.

to speak of it as if it were a mere shadow or negation of reality, so he was tempted by the Socratic identification of virtue and knowledge to explain away the fact of human responsibility. There is no avoiding this twist in Plato's teaching; he raises the point of irresponsibility again and again, and in one of the later books of the *Laws*, where, possibly, he is replying to certain criticisms of Aristotle,[12] he develops the thesis at great length and in such a way as to leave no room for misunderstanding. And, indeed, if we believe that all men do right so far as they know what the right is, and if we limit knowledge to what is learned by perception and experience, how shall we escape a kind of intellectual determinism? Instead of holding men responsible for their wilfulness, the Platonist in this sense should be one to say with Christ on the Cross, "Father, forgive them, for they know not what they do." As a matter of fact, Plato's common theory of punishment as purely remedial in function, rather than retributive, is quite in accordance with this view of human errancy; though it is to be noted that when he comes to deal with the practical details of criminal

E.g. Republic 412E

860D ff

Protagoras 323C ff
Laws 934A

12 Teichmüller's *Literarische Fehden* is replete with wild conjectures, but there is some plausibility in his contention that this excursus of the *Laws* is an answer to the strictures in the third book of the *Nicomachean Ethics* on the Socratico-Platonic thesis that no man errs, or sins, willingly.

procedure, he virtually allows a difference between voluntary and involuntary deeds of violence. Laws 865A

These inconsistencies of Plato with his own philosophy of free will and dualism cannot be shirked; nor should we forget that they have been the source, or encouragement, of a vast amount of twisted thinking on the capital question of evil and responsibility in Pagan and Christian writers. But, withal, it is still more important to remember that the burden of Plato's ethical feeling is prevailingly in harmony with his philosophy. No one was more conscious than he of the reality of evil, when his writing is free of entanglement in a rationalizing theodicy. The evil of life, he declares categorically, outweighs the good; and in general his tendency to err is rather on the side of an asceticism that exaggerates the conflict of principles in the soul. Republic 379C

And as with the reality of evil, so it is with the question of responsibility. No one can have followed the argument of *The Republic* without perceiving that the whole discussion of justice and injustice, happiness and misery, is based on a deep and unshakable consciousness of human responsibility. Nor are passages lacking that offer another explanation than intellectual determinism for the Socratic identification of virtue and knowledge. The principle of dualism is too firmly rooted in Plato's mind to permit him to dwell long in any rational evasion of reality. If you wish to look into his true heart, turn, for instance, to the opening of the fifth book of the *Laws,* where he proclaims roundly that to every man his whole being is double, and that all the honour and dishonour of the soul hang on the right recognition of this fact of consciousness: "For when a man holds not himself but others responsible for his various faults and for the many and great evils that befall him, and is always exempting himself as innocent, he is not really honouring his soul, as he thinks, but the very contrary." Ignorance and weakness may be regarded as the cause of evil, and are indeed the cause, if rightly considered, but behind them lies the original and mysterious power of self-love (*philautia*):

727B

Laws 731D

"The greatest evil to men, generally, is one which is innate in their souls, and which a man is always excusing in himself and so has no way of escaping. I mean what is expressed in the saying that every man is and ought to be dear to himself. Whereas the truth is that this absorbing self-love is continually and in all men the cause of all their faults; for the lover is blinded in regard to the object of his passion, so that he is a bad judge of the just and the good and the beautiful, always fancying that he ought to honour what belongs to him above the truth. Yet, really, he who would be a great man ought not to cherish himself or his possessions, but the things that are just, whether they pertain to himself or to the conduct of another. From this same fault arises the common habit of regarding our own ignorance as wisdom, and of thinking we know all things when, so to speak, we really know nothing."

These are words that should never be forgotten by the Platonist when Plato, for the moment, seems to sway from his own deepest convictions. They were, in fact, remembered and much quoted by the Platonizers of ancient Greece, especially by Plutarch. They may not, perhaps no words can, clear away the metaphysical difficulties that beset any one who, rashly or sullenly, undertakes to reason out the problem of evil, but they contain, I suspect, the only practical answer philosophy can give to that vexed question. It makes little difference whether we say that self-love is the source of ignorance and the evils that flow therefrom, or that ignorance is the source of self-love. Rather, the right way of proceeding is to grasp the distinction between the higher knowledge of intuition and the lower knowledge of things, which Plato so often makes, and, having firmly assured ourselves of this distinction, to see that self-love, as the spring of evil, is merely another name for the absence of the higher knowledge. Whether we call such a condition self-love or self-ignorance depends on whether we regard it from one or the other of the two contrary poles of the "self"; it is self-love if regarded from the lower element of our being, self-ignorance if regarded from the higher element. It is essentially, in the one case or the other, a failure to submit to the law of our double being, a kind of indolence, or want of attention, at the very centre of consciousness; for self-knowledge is the supreme activity of a soul attending to its own business.

Responsibility, then, is the word we use for that self-knowledge which tells us that the exercise or inertia of the inner check and the happiness or misery attendant thereupon are matters entirely within our own jurisdiction. But we also know that our pleasures and pains are contingent upon forces outside of our complete control; and here we are bound to hold ourselves creatures of fate and chance, and not responsible. In so far as the Socratic thesis may be taken to identify the higher knowledge and morality, it implies freedom and responsibility; in so far as it identifies practical knowledge and virtue it implies determinism and irresponsibility. To revert to the illustration employed by Plato and by Locke and Edwards, let us suppose the case of a man before whom liquor is set. On the one side he is drawn by a natural physical craving to drink; on the other side are the considerations of expediency and inexpediency which come to him in a more or less laggard manner from the memory of experience and from the precepts of tradition. If he exercises duly the will to refrain, so as to place himself in a position to form a clear image and judgement of the desirability or undesirability of drinking, he will be acting morally and will be happy; his judgement may be, probably will be, wise as well as clear, and the act of drinking or not drinking will probably result in pleasure; though there is also the possibility that his judgement may be based on insufficient knowledge, with the result of painful consequences. On the other hand, if he acts without due suspense of judgement, allowing himself to be hurried on by the physical craving or the contrary considerations without a proper balance of motives, and if his judgement is then erroneous, as it probably will be, he will not only suffer pain as a consequence of his action, but will feel that he has acted from self-love, or self-ignorance, and will be miserable accordingly. Whatever his course, he will be conscious that he was entirely free to exercise the will to refrain, or the inner check, and will hold himself responsible for his happiness or misery. But he will know also that, at the moment of action, his positive will was bound to follow the predominant inclination, and that, as the physical craving and the weight of experience were determined by causes not entirely within his jurisdiction, he is not fully responsible for the contingencies of pleasure and pain.

There is thus an element of responsibility in our conduct, and there is also an element of irresponsibility, and it was probably this complexity of our ethical nature that led Plato to waver in his attitude towards the question. And for the very reason that any philosophical statement of the problem must close with this admission of an irreconcilable paradox, Plato has, after his manner, given his final answer in the form of a myth, enjoying in this realm of symbols a release from the restricting law of scepticism. In the great epilogue to *The Republic* which describes the experience of men in the other world, it is said that the souls of the dead, after undergoing for a time the penalties and rewards of their former deeds, are brought together into the presence of the three Fates. Thereupon a prophet takes from the knees of Lachesis the various samples of lives and the lots, and from a lofty pulpit makes this proclamation: "The words of Lachesis, daughter of Necessity. Ye souls of a day, now is the beginning of another cycle of mortal life and death. Your daemon will not be allotted to you, but you shall choose your daemon. Let him who draws the first lot have the first choice, and the life he chooses shall be his destiny. But virtue is free, and as a man honours or dishonours her he will have more or less of her. The responsibility lies with the chooser; God is justified. Even for the last comer, if he selects wisely and will live diligently, there is ready a life, not evil, with which he may be content. Let not the first to choose be heedless, nor the last be dejected." So the lives are thrown down before the waiting souls, and the comedy of choosing proceeds. The moral of the allegory for us lies in the mixture of freedom and compulsion in the law. There is an element of hazard in the order and range of choice, yet Odysseus, the wise, to whom falls the last lot, seeks and finds the one life he desires, finds it lying neglected by all his predecessors.[18] The selection when it comes is the man's own, yet there is a bias in the soul which leads it to make a choice in accordance with its previous career. Only the few learn from past experience, and they so very little. The myth of transmigration was to Plato a half-serious parable of the same truth that was conveyed to the Hindu mind by the word *karma,* which meant at

[18] The combination of freedom and determinism, responsibility and irresponsibility, in Plato's myth became a subject of debate among the commentators. See Stobaeus, *Ethica* vii, 39.

once a man's voluntary deeds and their inevitable consequences, his freedom amid the coils of fate which he himself was weaving and could alone unravel:

> We harvest as the seed was sown,
> And he that scattered reaps alone;—
> So from each deed there falls a germ
> That shall in coming lives its source affirm.
>
> UNSEEN they call it, for it lurks
> The hidden spring of present works;
> UNKNOWN-BEFORE, even as the fruit
> Was undiscovered in the vital root.
>
> And he that now impure hath been
> Impure shall be, the clean be clean;
> We wrestle in our present state
> With bonds ourselves we forged—and call it Fate.[14]

[14] From *A Century of Indian Epigrams, chiefly from the Sanskrit of Bhartrihari.*

CHAPTER VI

THE DOCTRINE OF IDEAS

THE setting of the problem we have now to consider is admirably given in the introduction to the so-called *Moralia Magna* of the Aristotelian school. The first to approach the question of ethics, says the author of this treatise, was Pythagoras, who, however, erred in looking for virtues in numbers. After him came Socrates, who discoursed better and more copiously on these matters, but still faultily. For he placed the virtues entirely in the rational part of the soul, quite overlooking the irrational part and taking no account of the passions and the natural dispositions of men. The error is patent. In the sciences, when we know what a thing is we have the science. Thus, if a man knows what physic is, he is thereby a physician. But with the virtues it is not so; for it does not follow that, if a man knows what justice is, he is himself forthwith just. Afterwards Plato rightly divided the soul into two parts, the rational and the irrational, and distributed the virtues accordingly. So far well. But Plato also erred when he mixed up his discussion of virtue with his discussion of the Good as absolute truth and being; for there is nothing in common between these two questions. No doubt the good is the end and purpose of virtue, but this is the good as it is to us in our civil life, and not the Good conceived abstractly as an Idea separated from the actual things which we call good.

That is a fair summary of the ground on which Aristotle and later Peripatetics rested their opposition to the Platonic philosophy. It will be clear, I think, that their analysis of Plato's psychology was correct so far as it went, but was seriously inadequate. The more difficult problem remains, whether they were right in rejecting the doctrine of Ideas as an illogical sequence of psychological dualism. What were these Ideas, which have made such a stir in the world, and what is their exact place in the Platonic philosophy?

Now, it may be true that, looking into our souls, we are obliged to state the facts of consciousness in the terms of a paradoxical dualism, and such a statement may have great practical value, but it still leaves the facts, in one sense, quite unexplained. What is the bond between the inner check, or spirit, and the concupiscent element of the soul? How and why does the one act upon the other? How even can two essentially contrary powers exist together in one consciousness? These are the questions which reason thrusts upon a dualistic philosopher, and to which he can give no rational answer. The recourse to either form of monism he merely refuses as contradictory to the facts of consciousness, denouncing the acceptance of spiritual reality alone as a false idealism, and the acceptance of the concupiscent or sensational reality alone as a false scepticism. The attempt to bring the two terms closer together by lowering the spirit to a process of reasoning he repudiates as rationalism, and the effort to find some intellectual reconciliation of the irreconcilable he deals with as a futile presumption of metaphysics. Nevertheless, some sort of reconciliation the heart of man craves and will not, perhaps cannot, forgo; and the Platonic Ideas, as the dualist understands them, are primarily just the labour of the imagination to effect practically what could not be effected intellectually. We shall be in a better position to comprehend this act of the imagination when we have analysed Plato's treatment of a very complex subject.

The first and chief difficulty in the way of the interpreter is the obvious fact that Plato approaches the doctrine of Ideas from many different angles, and nowhere gives a final exposition of his meaning. That was his lordly privilege; so much so that one is sometimes tempted to believe, with Schleiermacher, that he deliberately left these obstacles in the path of his disciples in order that they might not be satisfied with the empty husks of word-knowledge, but should be kept aware of their ignorance until what they learned was illuminated by the light of their own inner experience. At any rate we should not fall into the error of smoothing away these obstacles by assuming a radical break in Plato's doctrine. That his attitude towards Ideas altered somewhat in the course of a long life may be granted; he would scarcely have been human if he had not suffered the changes of time. But to hold, as it has become rather the fashion nowadays, that at a certain moment in his career he repudiated one theory of Ideas and adopted a contrary theory, or even that the change in his views was anything more than the natural shifting of interest from one aspect of the question to another, is, I think, to misconceive seriously his philosophic history. The evidence for such a break is of the flimsiest sort and is contradicted by passages which can be explained away only by doing violence to the text.

If Plato appears inconsistent in his attitude towards Ideas it is because here, as in other cardinal points of his philosophy, he allows himself a puzzling license in the matter of terminology.[1] Sometimes the word "idea," or *eidos,* is used quite as it might be heard in the market-place, meaning simply the "form" of an object, or the "class" of objects grouped together more or less loosely by similarity of form; at other times it has a highly technical meaning as used in the schools; and it passes from one use to the other in such a way that on occasion we may have difficulty in determining its particular degree of technicality. But the most troublesome ambiguity—an ambiguity which has caused the spilling of oceans of ink and of some blood—meets us when we are most sure that the usage is strictly technical. It is hard for the classifying philologue or the systematizing metaphysician to acquiesce in the fact that the Platonic Ideas fall under two quite different categories corresponding to two different processes of the mind; and the maddening part of the truth is that Plato, though his whole philosophy hinges in a way on this distinction, will, when he pleases, write as if he were unaware of any such distinction. This sovereign indifference to our ease, I say, maddens the sytematizer and may blind the modest inquirer; yet the faithful Platonist would scarcely wish it otherwise, since he is thus

[1] It was a saying of the philosopher Didymus, as quoted by Stobaeus, that *τὸ πολύφωνον τοῦ Πλάτωνος οὐ πολύδοξον.*

forced always to remember the winged freedom of the spirit and the peril of scholastic pigeon-holes. What he might censure as ignorance or confusion in a lesser mind, he may tolerate as a not ignoble liberty in the proved seer. "A certain freedom in the use of words and phrases, with the avoidance of minute precision," Plato himself says, "is commonly allowed in a man who would not be pedantic; one even might call the contrary procedure illiberal."

Theaetetus 184c

The Ideas of Plato, then, fall under two main categories, which may be designated as the rational and the ethical. The former category is itself not simple, but must be taken to embrace both mathematical forms (the discussion of which we shall leave to the following chapter on Science) and those intellectual generalizations from particular objects to the group which are commonly, but erroneously, thought of first in connection with the Platonic doctrine. This second division, embracing intellectual generalizations, again falls into two subdivisions exemplified, respectively, by the Idea man which embraces within itself the many individual men we see, and the Idea table which we have in our minds in connexion with seeing and using many individual tables. In the one case the Idea is of a class of things in nature, and corresponds to the *genus* or *species* of modern science; in the other case it is of a class of manufactured objects. In either case the term, without question, has a certain practical utility and answers to a certain process of experience: that is to say, in common parlance we have no difficulty in distinguishing men as a group from any other group of animals, and tables from any other kind of furniture. The distinction is at least a pragmatical reality. Our minds are not harassed by the fact that creatures may be found or imagined which shade by imperceptible degrees upwards into men and downwards into apes, or by the fact that articles may be made which could with equal propriety be called tables or desks or shelves; for the ordinary concerns of life the distinctions are plain and the terms sufficiently precise.

But difficulties grow thick as soon as we begin to speculate. What is the nature of this Idea man or this Idea table which we have in our minds? Is it an entity apart from the individual objects, of which it is the pre-existent cause? And if so, how and where does it exist? Was it as an image in the mind of the Creator, or as a latent potentiality of impersonal energy, or as a pattern to which the Creator looked or which somehow controlled the impersonal energy? And how could there be a single stable image or potentiality or pattern of a group of individuals varying indefinitely in traits and merging insensibly into other groups? If there was a pre-existent Idea of men or tables, then why, by the same right, was there not an Idea of a certain class of men or tables, and then an Idea of a smaller group, and so on? Aristotle and other critics of Plato were not slow to bring out these difficulties. Of course we might say that it is just as easy to conceive the existence of an infinite number of Ideas as the existence of an infinite number of material objects, but we balk at the infinitude of Ideas as a needless duplicating of our troubles. On the other hand, if we reject Ideas as previously existent entities, and hold them to be no more than words corresponding to generalizations of the human mind, are we not bound by such a theory to reject also any principle of purpose or teleology in the world? The notion of purpose or design, whether we regard the world as created or self-evolved, can scarcely be maintained unless an Idea of what is to be unfolded already in some manner exists. Either course leaves us with insoluble difficulties, and hence the long and unended debate between the metaphysicians of the realistic and the nominalistic schools, between those who, in the medieval jargon, contended for *universalia ante rem* and those who contended for *universalia post rem*.

In a general way it may be said that with

natural classes, such as men and animals, the difficulties of the nominalistic view are seemingly the more insuperable, and that, in the slow return of science and philosophy to a dependence on some sort of teleology in the process of evolution, we are forcing ourselves back to a belief in Ideas in something like the Platonic sense. But with a manufactured article, such as tables, the obstacles in the way of accepting the Idea will seem mountainous; they loom up before the mind in the case of such an object because we see its conception and follow its construction as we do not in the case of natural groups. Some commentators, perceiving this difference in the difficulties, have urged that Plato held to Ideas of natural classes, but never, or only at an early stage of his mental development, believed in Ideas of manufactured articles. That is an old way with commentators, to strain at a gnat and swallow the camel. In reality the difference is apparent only and superficial, and it is just as easy to hypostatize one kind of generalization as the other. It ought to be perfectly clear from the tenth book of *The Republic*, if from no other passage, that Plato in his maturity held equally to both kinds of Ideas. It ought to be clear also that he spoke of Ideas as of entities anterior to individual objects and having an existence outside of the generalizing mind of man. To doubt this is to deny the plain sense of innumerable passages in his works and is to flout the common sense of many generations of readers.

So far the way of the interpreter is fairly clear and straightforward. He has simply to admit that Plato taught the reality of generalizations as preexistent entities, without attempting to explain the nature of their existence. In very sooth, there would appear to be no answer to such a question, and Plato himself was wise and honest enough not to stultify himself by trying to forge one.

He was saved from this intellectual stultification partly by his loyalty to the Socratic scepticism, and partly also, it may be, by the fact that his main interest lay not in these Ideas that correspond to generalizations from the similarity of objects of perception (nor even in those other rational Ideas, corresponding to mathematical forms, which are yet to be considered), but in Ideas (though he employed the same word for both kinds) of a different origin. It is hard to see how any one can read the Dialogues without being impressed by the fact that Plato was brought to his doctrine of Ideas by ethical rather than logical considerations, and that to the end, despite what may be called his period of metaphysical stress, his chief interest lay in this direction. The clue to his motives is given in the closing paragraphs of the fifth book of *The Republic,* where he is introducing his great argument on the place of Ideas in the philosophical and political life. What shall be our reply, he says, to the good fellow who is quite ready to admit the existence of beautiful things, but who laughs at us when we speak of the absolute unchangeable Idea of beauty as really and eternally existent apart from these particular things? Shall we not ask such a caviller to name any particular beautiful thing which on occasion may not appear ugly, or any just or holy act, so-called, which may not under other circumstances appear unjust and unholy? And so with other things we regard as great or small, heavy or light, and the like. No, the simple truth is that the popular ascription of beauty and the like is concerned with things that are tossing about in some mid-region between pure being and not-being; beauty and justice so taken furnish no hold on knowledge, neither can they be utterly ignored, but are matters of opinion only, a state of mind as shifting and uncertain as themselves. And as men use these words so will their hearts be. If a man admits the reality of beauty and justice as eternal Ideas he will love beauty and justice and embrace them as things he can know and depend upon; he will be a lover of such knowledge, a *philosopher.* But if he sees only a mutable world of things now fair and just, now ugly and unjust, he will perforce be content with this sort of uncertainty and will not endure to hear of fixed laws of beauty and justice. There is nothing for him really to know, no knowledge for him to love; he will not be a philosopher, but a lover of opinion, a *philodoxer*.

Now pretty much all of Plato's theory is in this passage, which I have given in somewhat condensed form, and it will repay minute study. In the first place it will be observed that the Ideas of great and small, corresponding to generalizations derived from the similarity of objects of perception, are thrown in among the Ideas of beauty and justice, as if all Ideas were of the same order. But their inclusion, it will also be observed, is merely casual, and they drop out of consideration when the value of Ideas is discussed and the necessity of their existence is maintained. This is in accordance with the common habit of Plato, to name together groups of intellectual and of ethical Ideas as if the argument were concerned with them indiscriminately, and then quietly to drop one or the other group. It is not the only case where he is content to draw tacitly, perhaps unconsciously, a distinction of prime importance to his philosophy.

It will be further observed that all through this argument, and indeed repeatedly in other Dialogues, Plato couples beauty with justice, or with goodness, as if they belonged to the same category; and in this case he does not name them together, merely to drop one of the classes, as he does when he includes intellectual generalizations with them, but maintains the union intimately to the end. There is here, then, a real refusal, or failure, to discriminate between aesthetics and ethics in the Ideal sphere. This, however, does not mean that he identified beauty and goodness through all their course, for there were many manifestations of beauty which he condemned as inimical to goodness; and it decidedly does not mean, as the Paterians would have us believe, that his primary interest was in the beautiful, for of such aesthetes he can on occasion speak with utter scorn. The explanation is, rather, that he made a distinction between Ideal beauty and the actual manifestations of beauty.

Laws 727D

Only once, in the *Hippias Major,* did Plato undertake to deal with the beautiful from a purely aesthetic point of view, and here the nearest approach to a definition, after many trials, is that beauty might be called "pleasure through sight and hearing." This definition, indeed, he finally rejects, because it does no more than describe the *effect* upon us of beautiful objects, whereas the beautiful itself, for which he is looking, would be

299B

the *cause* that brings together into a common category all the objects that so affect us. Yet it may stand as Plato's working definition of the beautiful, and fits in with his constant association of practical aesthetics and hedonism, the desire of beauty with the desire of pleasure. Beautiful objects as such are merely one division of things that give us pleasure, and are to be embraced or renounced, like all such things, not by a standard of immediate intensity but by a wider calculation of the kind of pleasure given. Other things being equal, the more beautiful object is preferable to the less beautiful, just as generally the intenser pleasure of the moment is preferable to the less intense. But "other things" are by no means always equal; the larger consideration of life may command us to condemn a particular manifestation of beauty, as it may bid us reject any other appeal to the senses, and above this fallible principle of hedonism is the moral law, with its power of inhibition upon the impulse of all desires. Hence it follows that art cannot be left to work under the canons of beauty alone, independently of outside control, but is to be judged by a standard embracing interests of far wider order; art must be subservient to ethics. In *The Republic* Plato, himself the master artist, shuts out of his ideal city poets and artists of high renown, men of whom he may elsewhere speak in the language of reverence, because the pleasure derived from their craft seems to his austere judgement contrary to the goal of happiness towards which he is straining. It is even true that he is wont to look with a touch of suspicion on art in itself, just as sometimes he is hurried by zeal, against his better judgement, to denounce pleasure in itself. He seems at these moments to feel that the tendency of art is almost inevitably to strengthen the immediate sensations against the inner check, and that there is an ancient irreconcilable feud between philosophy and poetry. This, however, is Plato troubled in spirit by too pressing a vision of the perils and misfortunes of life; in his calmer moods he recognizes the great function of art and poetry in education, and throughout the *Laws* there are passages on this topic replete with sound and subtle observation.

Republic 604D 606A, D

Ibid., 607B

But it is not my intention in this volume of introductory studies to enter into the complicated task of unravelling Plato's aesthetics, further than to show how and why that question is involved in the question of his ethics. In brief, the practice of art, as he saw it, is parallel with the practice of the virtues, but distinguished by the kind of pleasure evoked. When, however, we pass to the Idea behind the manifestations of beauty we are in the region of happiness, just as when we pass from considering the virtues to the moral force above them. And as happiness admits no distinction in kind, so the Idea of beauty merges into that of goodness. Hence there is no confusion, granted Plato's general point of view, as every true Platonist is ready to grant, in his method of dealing simultaneously with aesthetic and ethical Ideas.

But there is still another distinction to be made. (I trust the reader's patience is not exhausted; I sometimes fancy that the best definition of a Platonist would be "a lover of distinctions.") In the passage of the fifth book of *The Republic* to which we are referring, just before the paragraphs actually quoted, Plato speaks of the Ideas of justice and injustice, good and evil, each of which is one by itself, but by participation in acts and bodies and by communion one with another, has the appearance of being many. Now the point with which we are concerned is the inclusion of these Ideas of evil and ugliness (the latter, Ideas of ugliness, are not mentioned here, but they are so included in other passages of similar import) with those of goodness and beauty. Is the philosopher, then, as a lover of Ideas, one who loves ugliness and injustice by the same token that he loves beauty and justice? The answer to this question is

476A

implicit in the fact that here, as elsewhere, when Plato comes to draw his conclusions and apply his moral, he silently drops these so-to-speak reverse Ideas of ugliness and injustice out of consideration and argues as if he had named only beauty and justice. Ethically ugliness and injustice are not Ideas at all, denoting rather the absence of Ideas; but intellectually they may be called Ideas like any generalization of the mind, and as such they are, like other intellectual Ideas, listed with the ethical, and then tacitly ignored when the moral application is made.

It is clear, then, that in discussing Plato's doctrine of Ideas we have to deal with a very complex question. First of all we must set apart notions derived from the similarity perceived in a group of objects or from quantitative relations. With these must be placed also those aesthetic and ethical notions which are equally derived by generalizing from observation, and which include ugliness as well as beauty, unrighteousness as well as righteousness. All these are Ideas in a way and have their own reality; but they are intellectual in their origin and pertain to the scientific rather than to the philosophic life. The difference lies in this, that in the procedure of science we are interested in acquiring a knowledge of the Ideas, whereas in the procedure of philosophy we are interested in possessing the Ideas themselves. Ideas, as Plato was supremely concerned in them, and as they constitute the essence of what the world has rightly known as Platonism, are not derived intellectually, but are an emphatic assertion of the unchanging reality behind moral forces, a natural development of the Socratic affirmation of spiritual truth.

We can now understand why Plato saw in the rejection or acceptance of Ideas the line dividing men into two hostile camps. He had in mind one of the commonplace distinctions with which we are perfectly familiar today as were the people of Athens in his day, and which is fraught with far-reaching consequences. We are all acquainted with the man who, having a current knowledge of history and the world, insists fluently that there is no fixed standard of beauty or justice, and who overwhelms us with illustrations to prove that everything regarded as beautiful or just by one people and at one age is to another people or at another age the very reverse of beautiful or just. Plato would admit that such men, if the debate is kept within the bounds they prescribe, are measurably right; there is nothing absolutely fixed in particulars, and no knowledge of what is not fixed. But he would add that this is only the lower side of the truth. The fact that all peoples and all ages have some word, more or less precise, for the beautiful and the just, and have the same motions in their souls towards that which they call by these words, shows that some constant force is at work through all the variety of its manifestations. The objects and acts that appeal to an Australian headhunter as beautiful and right may in some respects be quite the contrary of what would receive the approbation of a Christian bishop; but beauty and justice, or rightness, have the same place and function in the soul of the one as of the other. These, Plato would say, are the absolute Ideas which both headhunter and bishop know, whereas in the application of these Ideas to particular objects and acts they fall into the region of opinion. Such, he would contend, is the fact, no matter whether you acknowledge it or not; but he would add that it matters a great deal to you personally whether you acknowledge it. If you admit the reality of the Idea of justice, you will love the Idea, and your love will be established upon something fixed; you will not only be confirmed in your readiness to act in accordance with the principles of justice as these are formulated by your own experience and by that of the society in which you live (whence all the practical virtues), but you will be led to search deeply into your consciousness for principles that approach more nearly to the absolute standard and authority of an Idea. You will be a promoter of your own welfare and of society's, a guide and governor among men who are groping towards wisdom, a philosopher. On the other hand, if you reject the Idea of justice and say there is nothing fixed and unalterable behind the changing fashions of law and custom, nothing at once the cause and goal of these fashions, if you say that justice is merely a name for acts which may have nothing in common, you are taking away all that gives to justice a firm hold upon the human heart. You will scarcely retain any deep love for what is only a name; you may conform to the popular rules of justice from habit or for prudential reasons, but, really, one may well be slow in trusting you very far out of sight, or in placing much reliance on your character—indeed, one may ask whether, properly speaking, you have such a thing as a character. If what is just today was unjust yesterday and may be unjust tomorrow, and if there is nothing behind these changes, one cannot see why you shouldn't change at your own convenience, without waiting for the slower-moving opinions of society. And certainly, supposing you are a lover of anything besides yourself, one cannot think of you as a philosopher, but, if you will pardon a rather ugly-sounding word, as a philodoxer.

These Ideas, then, which play so important a rôle in Plato's philosophy and have for these thousands of years haunted the world as impalpable embodiments of truth, are primarily ethical in their nature; and we have this pragmatic proof of their existence, that without them we can discover no sound basis of morality. They are, in fact, the very realities of our spiritual life, in comparison with which all the solid-seeming phenomena of earth are things evanescent and unreal. But in what does their reality subsist? What are they in themselves? To answer this question we must go back to the psychological analysis of morality.

The central truth of dualism is a recognition of the absolute distinction between the two elements of our conscious being, and an admission of the impossibility of finding any rationally positive explanation of the mutual interaction of these two elements. We know that our concupiscent soul is, or ought to be, under the jurisdiction of the spirit, yet our analytic reason can express this jurisdiction only in terms of suspension and an inner check. But the human mind cannot rest comfortably in this state of mere negation; it is impelled by its very nature to seek some positive expression for these superrational facts of consciousness, and it is just here that another faculty, the imagination, steps in to perform what was impossible to the reason. In its lower activity the imagination is the power by which the sensations derived through the organs of sight and the rest are projected outside of the mind as objects of perception. The imagination can also go beyond this function and, after recombining at pleasure the data of perception, can project these new combinations into the void as things having to the mind a certain degree of independent existence. Thus, the landscape conceived by the artist or the character conceived by the poet is thrown out into the world of objective existences. And so, by a still higher activity, the imagination essays to deal with the immediate data of consciousness, as it deals with those of sensation. Justice, which to the reason was only a negation of our positive impulses, is, like the creation of the artist, projected outside of the soul so as to become a positive entity with a life and habitation of its own, and the soul under control of moral force seems itself to be reaching out to touch and take into possession that to which it has given form and motion from its own experience.

These imaginative projections of the facts of moral consciousness are the true Platonic Ideas. Hence their peculiarity: though the most intimate realities of experience, things of which our knowledge is so firm and sure that of other things we seem in comparison to have only opinion, yet the moment we apply our discursive reason to them, the moment we undertake to describe them in intellectual terms, they melt away into nothingness, like the dew in the clear dry breath of the morning. Hence, too, the varying terms which Plato gives to their operation. They are always, as products of the imagination, objective entities, separate (*chôrista*) from the world of phenomena and from the soul itself, but at one time he may speak of them as patterns (*paradeigmata*), laid up in heaven or in some undefined region, to which we look as models to mould our conduct by, or, at another time, he may speak of them as visitants to the soul, neither exactly corporeal nor yet incorporeal, by whose presence (*parousia*) we possess the qualities of which they are the substance, or, more vaguely still, as mere forces (*dynameis*) that play upon us and make us what we are. The looseness of Plato's terminology would indicate that, to him at least, it is of relatively slight importance how we take them to be, so long as we accept their being and bow to their authority. The point of supreme importance for the Platonizer today is, not that he should be able to define the operation of Ideas, but that he should avoid the two contrary errors of the rationalist and the romanticist.

Sophist 247A

Ibid., 247E

On the one hand the literature of philosophy is replete with the ghastly failures of the rationalist, who, perceiving the illogical nature of these forms, has either rejected them and their author altogether in the name of reason, or, by attempting some intellectual "reconciliation," has reduced them to mere nominalistic categories of the reason and so emptied them of all vital significance. This denial of the office of the imagination is particularly the error of metaphysics, of which we shall have more to say in our discussion of the *Parmenides.*

But the other error is equally wide-spread and even more lethal in its consequences. I mean the error of the romanticist who sees clearly enough that Ideas are the property of the image-making faculty, but treats them as if they were somehow created by a purely spontaneous power *ex nihilo,* and so deprives them of eternal and authoritative validity. This is peculiarly the fault of the self-styled Platonists of modern times, but it may be traced back to the beginnings of romanticism, if not to the ancient school of Neoplatonists. Hegel laid his finger on one of its manifestations in his criticism of romantic irony: "It was Friedrich von Schlegel who first brought forward this idea, and Ast repeated it, saying, 'The most ardent love of all beauty in the Idea, as in life, inspires Socrates' words with inward, unfathomable life.' This life is now said to be irony! But this irony issues from the Fichtean philosophy, and is an essential point in the comprehension of the conceptions of most recent times. It is when subjective consciousness maintains its independence of everything, that it says, 'It is I who through my educated thoughts can annul all determinations of right, morality, good, &c., because I am clearly master of them, and I know that if anything seems good to me I can easily subvert it, because things are only true to me in so far as they please me now.' This irony is thus only a trifling with everything, and it can transform all things into show: to this subjectivity nothing is any longer serious."[2] But the evil has persisted in romantic writers who are serious enough in their way. It is not the misuse of Socratic irony, but a more subtle perversion of Platonic truth, which one will find, for instance, in such a writer as Professor Santayana, when he maintains that "religion and poetry are identical in essence, and differ merely in the way in which they are attached to practical affairs." By this he would argue, if I understand his drift, that the ideal world is a purely spontaneous evocation, and as in poetry every man is free to create what images he will, so it is in religion. "The impas-

[2] *History of Philosophy*, translated by E. S. Haldane, I, 400.

sioned soul," he says, "must pass beyond the understanding, or else go unsatisfied; and unless it be as disciplined as it is impassioned it will not tolerate dissatisfaction. From what quarter, then, will it draw the wider views, the deeper harmonies, which it craves? Only from the imagination. There is no other faculty left to invoke. The imagination, therefore, must furnish to religion and to metaphysics those large ideas tinctured with passion, those supersensible forms shrouded in awe, in which alone a mind of great sweep and vitality can find its congenial objects." But these Ideas are of the nature of things that cannot be verified. "Faith and the higher reason of the metaphysician are therefore forms of imagination believed to be avenues to truth, as dreams or oracles may sometimes be truthful, not because their necessary correspondence to truth can be demonstrated, for then they would be portions of science [that is, of what is known, in contrast with Ideas which would be matters of opinion], but because a man dwelling on those intuitions is conscious of a certain moral transformation, of a certain warmth and energy of life."[3] Now there is much in all this that seems to have the ring of true Platonism, but on closer investigation it will prove to indicate an attitude towards things of the spirit

[3] *Poetry and Religion*, pp. v, 6, 8.

which Plato would have met with scorn and denial. Plato would not say precisely with Santayana (we take him as typical of romantic Platonism) that the imagination *furnishes* to religion those large Ideas in which alone a great mind feels itself at home, but rather that the imagination gives vitality to the moral facts which are furnished it by religion. And Plato would have utterly denied that the correspondence of Ideas with truth cannot be demonstrated; on the contrary he would have asserted that the work of the imagination, unless it answers in the fullest measure to known truth, is not an Idea at all. Ideas are the product of the imagination, but of the imagination working upon material given to it by the immutable law of morality; the truth is present to our consciousness before this act of transformation, and has no more authority, though it may be clothed with more persuasion, after it has been evoked for the inner eye as a form than it had previously to that evocation.

I may seem to have dwelt overlong on this perversion, but the right use of the imagination is of the very essence of Idealism. It is true that the power of the Platonic philosophy over the minds and hearts of men is attributable in large measure to its insistence on the immediate vision of moral forces as Ideal entities; but it behooves the Platonist to remember also that the imagination is the most treacherous and headstrong of all our faculties if once it be permitted to slip the leash of moral control. The romantic spontaneity, which lures the imagination with a promise of irresponsibility in creating its moral and religious Ideas, is a meretricious parody of Platonism; its end is a bitter disillusion in the reality of misery. Alas that, surveying the many flatteries addressed to the soul under the guise of idealism, we must say in words that were so often in the mouth of Plato himself: How difficult are all things fair! How treacherous the desire of them!

Republic 497D

Such is the function, such are the limitations, of that activity of the soul which produces the Platonic Ideas. The name "imagination," I need scarcely add, does not itself occur in Plato, as indeed there is no word in classical Greek quite corresponding to its connotation; but I have not scrupled to apply our modern term to the process by which the ethical facts of consciousness are not only projected outside of the soul as independent entities, but are represented as images in some way visible. Vision, Plato observes, is the noblest of our perceptions, the sense that seems to bring us into closest intimacy with the objects of the phenomenal world; hence it is natural that, in the groping language of symbolism, our knowledge

Republic 507E

of Ideas should come to the soul by a spiritual organ similar in its operation to that of the physical eye. We see Ideas, Plato says, by the inner eye, "the vision of the understanding"—which is his nearest approach to a technical term for the faculty of the imagination regarded as a passive instrument. In the sixth book of *The Republic* (following the conclusion of the fifth book to which we have already referred) he elaborates the metaphor in detail, comparing the ethical Ideas in the soul with the models which an artist studies in the work of imitation. He is even so deeply convinced of the value of this similitude as to carry it beyond the mere usage of rhetoric into the region of mythology, as is his wont in matters that transcend the reach of rational definition. For is it, he would seem to ask, after all only metaphor? Does our imagination, as we think in our cooler moods, really create these Ideas as phantoms of its own evocation, or may it be that they are in fact bodied forms that show themselves to us in our moments of exaltation, creatures like to the gods who have their home on Olympus, yet at their own choice may be revealed to us in dreams or the more blessed hours of waking, recognized, for the dulness of our senses, only as they fade away into the air?

Symposium 219A

> By his pace in leaving us I knew,
> Without all question, 'twas a God; the Gods are
> easily known.[4]

And so we have the entrancing fable of the *Phaedrus,* wherein the Ideas are no longer described as images floating before the soul, but as shining realities, existing forever in their own light beyond the confines of the highest heaven. Thither the soul, when purified of her mortal passions, drives in her winged car with the lordly procession of the gods, and, reaching the apex of the skies, for the time of a celestial revolution looks out into those unearthly spaces, and beholds there the divine spectacle of justice itself and temperance itself, even knowledge itself, not as these things are guessed at in the shifting and uncertain phenomena descried by the purblind eyes of the body, but in their everlasting veracity and glory. That is the great and joyous feast of the soul—the eucharist of the philosopher, whereat he partakes of the eternal substance, and is made aware of his spiritual kinship with the gods. Is the fable a delusion, a mere hunger of the brain, the consolation of an innocent make-believe? How far, in other words, was Plato consciously turning his psychology into allegory, and how far did he regard his mythical account of Ideas as the shadow

[4] *Iliad* xii, 70, Chapman's translation.

of an immortal revelation? I for one would not care to say, holding that it is of the very essence of Platonism to leave these high matters in their own evasive liberty; but I know that Emerson wrote from the same true experience of the soul in his chapter on *Illusions:*

"There is no chance, and no anarchy, in the universe. All is system and gradation. Every god is there sitting in his sphere. The young mortal enters the hall of the firmament; there is he alone with them alone, they pouring on him benedictions and gifts, and beckoning him up to their thrones. On the instant, and incessantly, fall snow-storms of illusions. He fancies himself in a vast crowd which sways this way and that, and whose movement and doings he must obey: he fancies himself poor, orphaned, insignificant. The mad crowd drives hither and thither, now furiously commanding this thing to be done, now that. What is he that he should resist their will, and think or act for himself? Every moment, new changes, and new showers of deceptions, to baffle and distract him. And when, by and by, for an instant, the air clears, and the cloud lifts a little, there are the gods still sitting around him on their thrones—they alone with him alone."

And as the Platonic vision unrolls in a mythical space that is not the expansion of this world, so it falls in a time that is not measured by the interval between a man's birth and dying. The same magic of the imagination which placed the adventure of the soul in a region beyond the uttermost sphere of the heavens carries the event back to a remote age, to a life before the beginning of these terrestrial days. Our knowledge of Ideas, which now is of things at once visible and invisible, becomes by this act as it were a dim and transient memory of what the soul did veritably behold, face to face, in some prenatal existence. This is the meaning of metempsychosis and "reminiscence" as they are taught in the *Meno* and elsewhere, the setting in a mythical time and space of an experience which, philosophically considered, belongs to neither; for the Ideas, though known in time, are eternal, and though seen by the eye of the spirit, are not to be found among the phenomena that fill the boundaries of physical space. They are as the gods sitting on their unshakable thrones, seen through the drifting snow-storms of illusions.

He in whom the memory of this great adventure stirs is filled with longing to join the gods once again in their upward procession within the vault of the sky. So haunting is the recollection of his joy that in comparison with it all other satisfactions dwindle to worthless make-believe. Hence the theory of an Uranian love that carries the desires of the soul upwards to the participation in Ideas, like, yet very unlike, the common, or Pandemic, love that craves the pleasure of earthly possessions. In the greatest of the mythological Dialogues, the *Symposium,* Socrates tells a pretty tale which he pretends to have heard from the lips of an inspired woman of Mantinea. Love, he says, is not a god, neither is he a mortal, but a mighty daemon, begotten of the divine Poros, or Abundance, and conceived of the mortal Penia, or Penury, whose office it is to act as a mediator between gods and men. He it is that creates in us "the thirst that from the soul doth rise," the insatiable longings for wisdom, which is the most beautiful of all things. Such a desire is not known to the gods, for beauty and goodness in perfection are already theirs, and desire is only of that which is not possessed. Neither is it felt by the ignorant among men, for this is the very evil of ignorance that he who has no part in beauty or goodness or wisdom should yet be content with his lot; feeling no want, he has no desire. Love, the Uranian love, is philosophy; and the true philosopher is he who, having in memory the vision of the celestial images, possessing them yet not possessing them, feels the whole current of his being turned to the one supernatural desire to snatch them out of the shadowy past and make them the present palpable realities of his life. Every act, every wish, every thought, should be the perfect imitation, rather the complete embodiment, of an Idea. Imagination is not an empty dream, not a vacant and wandering liberty, but the master of things as they are and the moulder of his will.

It is this emotional element that distinguishes the Platonic philosophy from the other schools, and has made it an undying force in the practical world; and this emotional element must be regarded, I think, as the indispensable servant of truth, if philosophy is to be a life and not an idle disputation. But I dare not say that it has passed into wide acceptance without bringing grave perils in its train. Plato himself may have taken great pains to discriminate theoretically between the love of Ideal beauty, which is akin to the love of endurance and temperance and wisdom and all the chorus of the virtues, and the other love which is not Ideal at all, but a license of the imagination or a lust of the flesh; but it needs a strong man to maintain such a distinction, when all the powers of the world, together with the subtler power of self-love, make for confusion. It is thus not without reason that Platonic love has often passed into a jest, and sometimes into a reproach. Nor can Plato for this be held entirely guiltless. There are passages of the *Symposium,* and more particularly of the *Phaedrus,* in which the passionate colour of his language so envelops the allurement of particular objects that some effort of the mind is required to remember the Ideal beauty of which they are supposed to be the manifestations. The danger is heightened when he speaks with curious lack of indignation of pleasures which the world has agreed to hold unnatural and to reject with instinctive abomination. Yet in these few isolated passages where the attraction of sensuous beauty seems for the moment to have veiled his purer ethical vision, we do him a great wrong if we fail to remember that it is a passing cloud before the sun of the soul, not an eclipse. We need then to turn to the strange confession of Alcibiades at the close of the *Symposium,* and to learn again how rigidly beauty and all the seductions of pleasure were held in subjection to the refraining will. The Socrates of Plato may have portrayed himself playfully as a slave to any beautiful body and as wise only in erotic lore; when it came to the test of action he could master the lawless impulses of the flesh unflinchingly and, as it seems, without a pang of regret. Those who dwelt with him and understood his manner of speech knew well enough that all his babble about the pursuit of beautiful bodies was but a veil of irony thrown before the hunger of his soul for fulfilment of its unearthly love.

Theages 128B

Symposium 216D

The Ideal world, created or, it may be, obscurely grasped by the imagination, is thus at once an illusion and a reality, with this difference, that when we deal with philosophy as a mere dead corpus of speculation these Ideas fade away into an illusory make-believe, whereas such is the constitution of our spiritual nature that the more we take philosophy as a principle of life the more vivid and real do they become. That is a truth which can be demonstrated only by living, not by argument. But of the facts of ethical experience underlying the Ideas there is no such halting tale, no question at all of make-believe. Here we have not to do with the metaphorical "eye of the understanding," but with that form of progressive knowledge, rather with the only immediate and veritable knowledge, which Plato designated as dialectic—that is, the philosophy of the soul discoursing with herself of the pure intuitions of consciousness, and so passing ever upwards to larger and more comprehensive truth. The parallel processes of that ascent, dialectical and Ideal, may be described somewhat as follows. Let us suppose that a certain pleasure is presented to a man. His natural desire is forthwith to reach out for this pleasure; but he is made to pause. This power of suspension, which to Locke was the substitute for the free will, and which I have termed the inner check or, more precisely in the language of Plato, the daemonic opposition, intervenes between desire and the reaching out for fulfilment. The man has time to calculate from experience or precept, half unwittingly it may be, whether it will be better to grant himself this pleasure or to forgo it. The result of this act of suspension, whether it end in permission or negation, and whether the judgement of ultimate pleasure and pain be right or wrong, is the virtue of temperance, and with it comes the feeling of happiness. That is the dialectical certainty, what we know by immediate and incontrovertible evidence. But with this certainty there rises before the man's imagination, if he reflects on his state, the Idea of temperance as a visible power or presence, so alluring in itself that beside it the object of his physical desire appears mean and ephemeral. If his judgement was led to veto that desire it will seem to him that his act of restraint was merely the choice in its place of this more desirable image; the love of the Idea has driven out the baser love of the flesh. If his judgement granted the desire as good, then it will seem to him as if this desired object were indeed beautiful, but beautiful only as a shadow or receptacle of the overflowing loveliness of the Idea.

Now suppose this event of the soul, if I may so call it, is followed, as in life it will be, by other events in which various desires more or less similar in nature are involved. Out of the grouping of these events will arise a larger experience of the happiness invariably attendant on the inhibiting power and a clearer consciousness of this power itself as the determining element of the soul's true welfare. We grow thereby in dialectical knowledge. And with this growth there follows a like enlargement of the ethical imagination. The Idea of temperance comes to embrace more details and fuller reality, and to show on its face a more radiant charm; and as our love of the Idea is enhanced, the desire of any particular pleasure dwindles in comparison. With larger dialectical knowledge the Idea of temperance is taken up into a more comprehensive form, into the Idea of fortitude, it may be, as the soul's virtue of resistance to all temptations, whether of desire or of aversion, hope or fear; and this Idea again may be carried up into the still larger Idea of wisdom, and ever onward to the supreme Idea of the Good.

Symposium 211C

And so, as it were by the steps of an ascending stairway, we have reached the summit of Plato's dialectic and of human experience, to that Idea of the Good which to the practical mind of the writer of the *Moralia Magna* seemed a fantastic unreality, but to the inward-looking eye of the soul is the one supreme reality. It is not to be wondered at that certain of Plato's contemporaries were made dizzy by the attempt to gaze directly at this luminary of truth, as the eye of the body is blinded by meeting the unveiled radiance of the sun, or that tradition should have soon gathered strange tales about the lectures in which he unfolded his theories.[5] Plato himself virtually admitted that no definition of the Good was possible, since there is nothing beyond it from which further light could be obtained, and there is no way of explaining why we desire that which is the end of all desiring. The only device for turning the eye of the soul thitherward is not by endeavouring to define the undefinable, but by pointing out the direction to be taken by those who would approach it; as Plato has done symbolically in the wonderful allegory of the cave, and, more analytically, in the discussion, following this allegory, of the propaedeutic training in abstract thought.[6] It is possible that in the lectures devoted to this preliminary training Plato may have been careless in his use of terms, but two things are certain: the alleged confusion of his mathematical with his ethical Ideas, on which Aristotle laid so much

Republic 506D

Republic Bk. vii

5 For example, the often-quoted story of Aristoxenus, *Elements of Harmony* ii, 30.

6 The scholium to *Gorgias* 506c puts the case well: "For the Good, as the end, is in itself undefinable. Wherefore it is here set forth by means of negation of what it seems to be, as for instance that it is not pleasure." And so on of its treatment in other Dialogues.

stress, is, as we shall see in our study of Plato's science, a disastrous misunderstanding of his method; and the tradition of an esoteric doctrine, as distinct from the supposedly popular exposition of his philosophy in the Dialogues, has not the slightest foundation in fact. The Dialogues, as we have them, carry the mind as far as it can go, further than most minds are willing to follow, and the notion of a secret truth still beyond is merely the hugger-muggery of an age which was losing its power to discriminate between thinking and wishing to think. What, in the name of intelligence, should that mystical doctrine be? If there were no other damning evidence, the silly allusions to this enigmatic teaching and the statement that Plato never had written and never would write down his true principles are sufficient to prove the so-called Platonic Epistles a forgery.[7]

But if we cannot define the supreme Idea—since it is the ethical fact which must be used to give meaning to all our ethical definitions—at least we can look at it, as Plato did, from different points of view. What it is not we can say with assurance. It is not pleasure, since pleasures may be relatively either good or bad. Neither is it

Republic 505BC

[7] Ch. Huit, *La Vie et l'oeuvre de Platon*, I, chap. v, §§ 7 and 8 (the two sections by an oversight are both numbered 7), has dealt magisterially with the subject of these lectures and of an esoteric doctrine.

knowledge, in the ordinary sense of the word, since those finer wits who would so define it are obliged in the end to say "knowledge of the Good." How, then, shall we approach it positively?

When we see the supreme Idea, or seem to see it, as a power at work in other things than ourselves, in the material world first of all, and then in the characters of men as a part of that visible world, we call it Beauty. And so we have the marvellous account, in the *Symposium*, of the upward progression of the soul when, drawn by the charm of a fair form, she passes on to consider this form with other fair forms, and from these to fair actions, and from these to fair notions, and out of these to that one notion of absolute beauty, and catches glimpses of Beauty at last as it is in itself. This, be it observed, is not the surrender of the soul to the allurements of gold and rich vestments and the physical bloom of youth, which might lead us in a direction the very opposite of the Good, but is, as it were, a rejection of these attractions while in the act of appreciating them. It is not, as in the case of the mere aesthete, a submersion of the soul in the flux of the world as the flux appears to us stayed and informed by a force equivalent to the inner check, but an invigorating sense of this force as so manifesting itself in the world and as drawing us by the world, and from the

211c ff

world, to itself. And he who thus rests his eyes upon the divine indwelling force of beauty, rather than upon its scattered and inert manifestations, will feel awakened within himself a kindred impulse, not of passive pleasure, but of moral energy, spurring him to engender true deeds of virtue, as an immortal being raised into the companionship of God.

With that last word we see how easily the supreme Idea passes into the field of religion. The apex of our aesthetic experience which was attained by the ascending steps of generalization is now regarded as the model upon which God himself sets his eyes when He reaches down into the world and imposes upon its fleeting substance the forms and order of stability. And so the Idea of the Good, which at one moment seemed to Plato almost the active Cause of being, as contrasted with the not-being of chaos, will become to him, particularly in his later years when in the *Timaeus* and the *Laws* he turns from the vexations of metaphysical inquiry back to the less inquisitive faith of youth, simply God; not the gods of the popular pantheon whose story is filled with the evils and atrocities of human lawlessness, but the God who is as it were the reflection in the mirror of the universe—it may rather be the original and no reflection at all—of that daemonic check in the soul which is the cause of truth and beauty.

But withal, however large a part we may suppose the supreme Idea to play in our aesthetic and religious life, it was still more important, in Plato's philosophy, to study it there in the soul itself. For thus alone we shall not infer it by metaphor or allegory, but know it, know it immediately in its pure essence, as that for which all other things are desired and which is the end of all desire—the Good. And how do we know that which surpasses knowing? The answer was given by Plato in the argument of *The Republic;* it may be found summarily stated in an early Christian theologian who was often a better Academician than were the Pagans who usurped the name: "Plato himself says that happiness (*eudaimonia*) is the well-being of the daemon, and that by the daemon is meant the governing element of our soul, and that the most perfect and fullest Good is this happiness."[8]

In this consummation of Plato's dialectic we see how at last the three theses that wind in and out of his Dialogues are brought together and indissolubly united. The Good is the spiritual

[8] Clemens Alexandrinus, *Stromata,* II, xxii, 131. Αὐτὸς δὲ ὁ Πλάτων τὴν εὐδαιμονίαν τὸ εὖ τὸν δαίμονα ἔχειν, δαίμονα δὲ λέγεσθαι τὸ τῆς ψυχῆς ἡμῶν ἡγεμονικόν, τὴν δὲ εὐδαιμονίαν τὸ τελειότατον ἀγαθὸν καὶ πληρέστατον λέγει.—cf. *Timaeus* 90c.

affirmation of Socrates, spoken now in the tested language of philosophy. It is the scepticism of Socrates, since it states a fact that cannot be defined in the terms of the understanding, and bids the reason submit to this fact as to a master. In its double aspect it is the solution of the Socratic paradox, since with the soul's own feeling of happiness it makes moral intuition the one certain thing above peradventure, thus identifying morality and knowledge, while as the source of what light we have to guide us in the practical decisions of this world, it imparts a measure of truth to our judgements and the power of judging to the mind, thus identifying virtue and right opinion. It is the limit of self-consciousness, given by the soul to the imagination, and rendered by the imagination back to the soul as an Idea, "more beautiful than truth or knowledge."

Republic 508E

CHAPTER VII

SCIENCE AND COSMOGONY

WITH his habitual flexibility Plato, as we have seen, used the term "Idea" both for the rationalized forms of things in time and space and for the moral intuitions of the soul. The latter are the field of true dialectic, or philosophy, the former of intellectual dialectic, or science; and the failure to discriminate resolutely between these two fields has been a fruitful source of error among self-styled Platonists from the beginning down to the present day. The confusion is in some measure attributable to the fact that Plato had at command no specific word corresponding to our conception of "science," but, as in Latin, so in Greek, the same general expression (*scientia, epistêmê*) had to do duty for all kinds of knowledge. The chief task of the commentator, therefore, may sometimes seem to be nothing more than the imposition of a rigid terminology on the freer method of the Master. The process, one admits, is not without its dangers, similar to those that attend the hardening of religious faith into formulated creeds; but the risk is necessary, in the one case as in the other, if we would guard ourselves against the heresies that seek authority under the cover of a great name.

In the introductory books of *The Republic* Plato showed that a State is rightly governed when there is a proper division of the citizens and when each class performs its own duties, one class guiding, another defending, another producing. In like manner an individual man is in a healthy condition when his various faculties function normally. Both the State and the man, when so functioning, possess the several virtues of wisdom, courage, and temperance, belonging respectively to the separate classes and faculties. In both, justice is regarded as the active principle which, by its power of temporary or permanent veto, holds each class or faculty to the performance of its particular duty; it is the dynamic centre of morality manifesting itself at the periphery in the specific virtues. Now this healthy condition can be assured only by that complete self-knowledge which will place philosophy in command of the soul and the philosopher at the head of the State. What, then, is the procedure by which we shall attain to this knowledge? Manifestly it is by means of a course of education directed not so

Republic 518c

much to the acquisition of crude information (Plato accepted the old Greek saying that "much-learning does not educate the mind") as to the end of turning the whole soul from the pursuit of shadows to the contemplation of the one light of truth.

It is at this point, before entering upon the intellectual discipline necessary for the philosopher, that Plato introduces the famous image of the divided line, the nature of which can be best displayed in a diagram, thus: 509D ff

Opinion		Knowledge	
Conjecture	Belief	Understanding	Pure reason, Knowledge
Images, Reflections, etc.	Objects, Animals, etc.	Mathematical forms	Ethical experiences

At a first glance the main bifurcation here is that between the two great fields covered the one by opinion, with its two grades of conjecture and belief, and the other by knowledge, with its two corresponding grades; and this, indeed, is a dichotomy that runs all through Plato's works—on the one side the uncertain mutability of the phenomenal world and of our relation to it, on the other side the certain stability of the intelligible world. Yet, as we follow the application of his line to the actual system of education, we discover that the emphasis of division undergoes significant changes. To begin with, the first of the four members, that of images and conjecture, is quietly dropped out of consideration, though, for other purposes, it is taken up again in the last book of *The Republic*. This leaves us with a threefold division of material objects, mathematical forms, and ethical experiences, which, it will be seen at a glance, correspond to the three classes of Plato's Ideas. Now, as Plato is dealing here with education as a discipline in the knowledge of Ideas, we should expect this triple classification to redivide so as to indicate two main groups, embracing on one side those generalizations from particulars and those mathematical forms which together are the subject matter of science, and on the other side those intuitions which belong to the true dialectic. And such is the case; Plato's line does ultimately conform to this fundamental dualism of his philosophy, although the fact is obscured somewhat by the peculiar bent of his mind.

In his conception of science, contrariwise in this to his ethical procedure, Plato shows everywhere a strong bias towards the deductive method; and as a result his comparative contempt for pure observation and for generalization by induction led him to neglect the experimental and biological bases which Aristotle did so much to establish. Even the mania, as it might almost be called, for classification which infests some of his later Dialogues—notably the *Sophist* and the *Politicus*—does not work itself out by an inductive ascent from the less inclusive to the more inclusive, but proceeds downward by a series of rather mechanical dichotomies. It follows that the parts of science admitted into his educational curriculum are preponderantly the deductive branches of mathematics, beginning with arithmetic and passing on through plane and solid geometry to astronomy and musical harmony. Though the Ideas corresponding to natural *genera,* which are treated in the inductive sciences, may not be excluded absolutely from such a scheme, they will sink to a very subordinate position.

In determining the place of astronomy and music—more particularly the former—in such a curriculum, Plato raises the question whether the method of study then in vogue should not be changed for one better suited to the purpose of philosophical training, and to this end he emphasizes the difference between the mere observation of phenomena and the pursuit of scientific, or mathematical, law. All these devious lights which we behold moving in the sky are indeed the fairest and most orderly of visible objects, yet are far from those true motions and those exact forms apprehensible by the understanding alone and not

Republic 529C, 531B

by the eyes. They are to be used as rough diagrams written out for us in the heavens and serviceable to the reason, but the geometer, though acknowledging their excellence as works of handicraft, would deem it absurd to study them seriously as if in them could be found the absolute laws of proportion. Now, some part of this contempt for the slower procedure of observational science must be laid, as we have said, to Plato's ineradicable distrust for things as they are and to the deductive bias of his mind; but in a measure also it can be ascribed to the imperfection of the available means of observation. The astronomer of that day possessed no mechanical instrument by which the motions of the celestial bodies could be accurately observed and so made the basis of mathematical formulae. Hence the scientific astronomer (in Plato's sense of the word) would be obliged to work upon an intellectualized sphere, so to speak, of which the visible scroll of the heavens is a clumsy and everchanging imitation. In this notion of a mathematical system which could be guessed at from what was actually observed, Plato was looking beyond his age to the time when the real science of astronomy was possible; but we may suppose also that, if he were living today, he would still hold it a form of illusion to believe that the relations of material phenomena of any sort are such as can be contained in a complete equation. He would maintain that there is no perfect correspondence but only an approximation between the facts of observation and the generalized laws which belong rather to the apparatus of our own intelligence; and in this, I take it, he would be in accord with the most recent trend of scientific theory.

Observational astronomy Plato, therefore, relegated to a place among the arts, and rejected its pretensions to the name of science. The higher education of the philosopher was not concerned with those Ideas which correspond to generalizations from particular objects such as men or tables, or from the visible motions of phenomena, even the majestic phenomena of the heavens, but with those Ideas of form and quantity and time which belong to the pure understanding; not with the stars and their measured orbits, but with the absolute circles and ellipses of an immaterial world. Yet this Ideal science, all science indeed, is only a part of the propaedeutic to the veritable interest of the philosopher; we reach at last the essential division in Plato's scheme. To comprehend this bifurcation we must recur again to the fourfold line in which the progress of education was figured, and must take note of a curious ambiguity in its terminology.

Under the higher division of "knowledge," as distinguished from "opinion," are embraced two fields: one of mathematical forms and the corresponding faculty, or understanding; the other of ethical experiences and the faculty corresponding to these, which, among its various appellations, is called by precisely the same term, "knowledge," as that under which both of these spheres are subsumed. That is to say, we are brought once more face to face with the troublesome fact that Plato recognized two kinds of knowledge (entirely apart from the realm of opinion), and that in some passages he treats these as if identical, while in other passages the central thesis of his philosophy seems to depend on maintaining a distinction between them.

Certainly this distinction is made with formal precision, and the relative places of science and dialectic are settled without ambiguity, in the closing paragraphs of the sixth book. Students of arithmetic and geometry, it is there said, assume the odd and even forms, the three kinds of triangles, and the like as universally admitted hypotheses which need no proof, and from these proceed to demonstrate whatever problem they have in view. They use, indeed, visible figures in these demonstrations, but in reality their concern is with the absolute square, for instance, or the

Republic 510c ff

absolute diagonal, which exist in the understanding alone and of which the diagrams drawn by them are only symbols. This procedure belongs to the intelligible sphere of knowledge, although in it the soul cannot rise to first principles but is obliged to cling to hypotheses, employing for this purpose the intellectualized figures of material objects. Such is the sphere of geometry and the other mathematical sciences. In contrast with this is the higher sphere of the intelligible (the highest of the four divisions). Here, reason starts indeed with hypotheses, as it does in science, but uses them merely as a point of departure for its ascent into a world that is above hypothesis, and so mounting climbs to the first principle of all (the Good). This is the world of knowledge and true being contemplated by dialectic (that is, *ethical* dialectic, as shown in Plato's practical illustrations, though he does not here so qualify it), a clearer and purer world than that of the sciences so-called. The activity of the mind concerned with geometry and its cognates is properly termed understanding and not reason (the higher reason, or intuition), as falling between opinion and reason.[1]

I do not see how it could be averred in plainer

[1] Republic 511D: *Διάνοιαν δὲ καλεῖν μοι δοκεῖς τὴν τῶν γεωμετρικῶν τε καὶ τὴν τῶν τοιούτων ἕξιν ἀλλ' οὐ νοῦν, ὡς μεταξύ τι δόξης τε καὶ νοῦ τὴν διάνοιαν οὖσαν.*

language that the essential division of the line marks off dialectic alone on the one side, and on the other side the three fields of which mathematics and its abstractions are the highest. And the value of science, as of the departments below it, is not in itself, but in its use as a gymnasium, or training place, for the mind that is preparing for the philosophic life. Each study, beginning with the common arts, is an illustration, so to speak, of that above it; practice of the lower faculty is a discipline for the exercise of the higher, while the potential presence of the higher demonstrates itself in the activity of the lower. There is nothing of the "ivory tower" in this system, no place for the dreamer in wisdom or for the antinomian hypocrite; and Plato is as thoroughly convinced as St. James that faith and works cannot be disjoined. How otherwise could it be in a doctrine wherein the assurance of truth takes the form of happiness attending an active and unremitting self-government? And so, however sharply Plato's philosophy in its logical aspects falls into an absolute dualism, in practice it is always presented as a slow ascent of the soul by the steps of physical and mental and moral discipline.

Republic 535B *ante et post*

If, in the course of education just described, the mathematical sciences seem to have usurped an undue prominence, our judgement of the fact must take various considerations into account. In the first place it must be remembered that the training of the body and the ordinary instruction in the arts had already been discussed by Plato at great length in earlier books of *The Republic*. And, secondly, mathematical studies were the only ones sufficiently advanced in Greece to offer the sort of discipline obtained in our graduate schools today in many fields of history and linguistic beyond the preparatory and general education of the college. But even if this were not the case, it is probable that Plato would have regarded studies of which geometry is the type as peculiarly adapted to the immediate preparation for the life in philosophy towards which all serious education was directed. For mathematics, like dialectic, deals with unchanging realities, though in a different sphere of the Ideal world; and by our experience with the fixed hypothetical abstractions of mathematics Plato would hold that we are helped to rise above a dubious recognition of the shifting standards of custom and tradition into loyalty to the eternal veracity of ethical Ideas.

Furthermore, and this, perhaps, is the real key to Plato's exaggerated interest in the science of number, mathematics rests finally on the basis of the one and the many, abstracting from the per- 525D ception of the divisible one and the unifiable many the conception of an absolute One and an absolute Many. And this distinction between unity and multiplicity, the uniform and the various, the unchanging and the changing, the self-complete and the progressive, at once abstract and corresponding to actual experience, is the only resource at our command to express in language of the understanding the ultimate dualism (as we thus call it) of consciousness upon which morality is founded. With this instrument at his disposal, the dialectical philosopher is able to give an account of himself, and to ward off delusive notions and the attacks of false logic. He not only possesses the faith of intuition, but is armed with the full panoply of discursive reason. In Socrates Plato saw the perfect model of such a dialectical gladiator.

The Dialogue in which Plato develops his scientific theories in connexion with a vision of the universe as a whole is the *Timaeus*. I suspect that most students who approach this strange piece of writing will undergo an experience somewhat as follows. A first reading is likely to leave them merely confused and mystified. A second reading will lead them to feel that part of the Dialogue, the religious speculation, contains a sublime allegory, while another part, the scientific speculation, still repels them as futile and wearisome. A third reading may bring the conviction that even this scientific speculation, though in detail often resting on hasty assumptions and missing the inductive method of experiment, is yet as a whole one of the very great achievements of the human brain. Certainly the attempt to reduce the material universe to a purely geometrical and mechanical system has allured thinking men from that day to this, with, it must be added, utterly different results according as they have been true or not to the spirit in which Plato himself conceived the function of science.

Whatever may be doubtful in the interpretation of the *Timaeus,* one thing ought to be beyond question: the whole argument is founded on a radical dualism. To say, with the English editor, that here we find "Platonism as a complete and coherent scheme of monistic idealism,"[2] is to suffer the error, only too common at the present day, of forcing into Plato's words a metaphysic which is quite contrary to their plain meaning. The true thesis is stated unequivocally in the opening sentences of the argument: "In the first place, then, in my opinion, we must distinguish these two things: What is that which always is and has no becoming, and what is that which, always becom- 27D

[2] Archer-Hind, *Introduction,* p. 2.

ing, never is? The one, being always the same, we comprehend by thought with reason; the other, becoming and perishing, never really being, we guess at by opinion with unreasoning perception." And this distinction is repeated at the opening of the second main division of the argument: 47E "What we have said hitherto, with slight exceptions, was concerned with exhibiting the things created through mind, or reason; but we must now add to our exposition the things that become 51D out of necessity. . . . If reason and true opinion are two things different in kind, then do the unchangeable Ideas surely exist as objects of reason alone, not perceptible by our senses; but if, as some hold, true opinion differs in nothing from reason, then all that we perceive by our bodily organs must be regarded as having the most real existence."

That is to say, in both the grand divisions of the argument the starting-point is the immediate consciousness of that dualism within the soul itself which, intellectually, appears as knowledge and opinion; and from this the assumption is made that the world of which we are members must conform in some way to this double operation of consciousness. If we have reason, a certainty of knowledge, there must exist in the universe at large a sphere of changeless, eternal objects which can thus be known, the Ideas, and these must be absolutely different in kind from the objects of physical perception which have the changing, ephemeral nature of opinion. The cosmogony of the *Timaeus* will be a marvellously unrolling picture of the relation and interaction between these two elements, a supreme effort of the imagination working out the story of creation, not in capricious license, but under the control at each step of the law of our own inner being—at least such ought to be the procedure, and such the procedure is when Plato remains true to his own law of scepticism.

At the centre of this story lies the great passage, already quoted as one of the mottoes of this book, which, more clearly perhaps than any other words in Plato, states the purpose and character of his philosophical investigation: "Wherefore we must discriminate between two kinds of cause, the one of necessity, the other divine: and the divine cause we must seek in all things, to the end that we may possess a happy life so far as our nature permits; and the necessary cause for the sake of the divine, reflecting that otherwise we cannot apprehend by themselves those truths which are the object of our serious study, nor grasp them or in any other way partake of them." Such is the double aspect of the world, a divine

68E

element and a substratum of brute necessity, as reflected in the dualism of our own souls; and the tale of creation is divided accordingly into two sections, as the work is considered to proceed from above downwards or from below upwards.

In the first account, taken in briefest outline, we are told how God creates the actual world as a living animal in likeness of the Ideal world. As to the manner in which Plato conceives this Ideal model of which our universe is the imperfect, but the best possible, imitation, there is no clear statement; the conception is left in the same mythical penumbra that always surrounds his theory of Ideas. Are these Ideas, we ask, the thoughts of God, or are they eternal laws, or substantial entities of some sort existing outside of himself; and there is no definite reply. The like insoluble question, whether holiness and righteousness are determined by God's will or themselves determine 100 it, was raised in the *Euthyphro,* as it has been raised since by Christian theologians and left unanswered. In a general way we may say this: that the conception of Ideas runs parallel in Plato's mind with the mythology of a vaguely personal deity; when the mere immanence of the divine in the phenomenal world, or the similarity of the phenomenal to the divine, is dominant in his thought, then the divine floats before his vision as the Ideal, and he speaks as a philosopher; but when the divine is considered rather as an energy or cause working upon brute material and moulding it as a man shapes an image to his will, then he is wont to speak in theological language of God, the creator and upholder and judge.

Having created this world-soul and its vehicle, God then from what remains of the soul-stuff fashions the immortal souls of men, which He distributes to the stars, where they are indoctrinated in the knowledge of their destiny and duty. Thereupon he rests, and calls upon the lesser gods to fashion the various mortal creatures in their kinds, leaving this task to his lieutenants lest any one should impute to the hand of the supreme Demiurge the imperfections that must inhere in transitory things. First his delegates compose the lower soul of man. To reason, which is placed in the brain and so separated from the other two faculties and from the influence of the grosser body, they add the *thymoeides* (seat of the personal emotions), which goes to the breast, and is generally an assistant of reason in governing the third faculty; and then this third faculty, the concupiscent element, situated in the abdomen. As in *The Republic,* the significant division is between reason, which is divine and immortal, and the emotional and concupiscent members of the soul, which are mortal and often indistinguishable from the body.

The second part of the Dialogue takes up the story of creation from the material side. The substratum of the world, upon which the Demiurge and his delegates work, is described as the expansion of space, or the irregular and unresting flux, which is brought into comparative order by the imposition of limits and geometric forms. We have thus the fundamental dualism falling into a counterpart of the fourfold scheme of the *Philebus:* at the one extreme is the "cause," or God, at the other extreme the "infinite" (*apeiron,* more properly the limitlessness of chaos than our notion of infinity); and between them the irrational relation of these two extremes, expressed as the "limit," or mathematical form, and the "limited," or formal world. But for the infinite of the *Philebus* Plato substitutes in the *Timaeus* a term of wider and deeper significance. This substratum of the limitless flux is now called by the name "necessity" (*anankê*), which points at once to the double aspect of creation that was always more or less clearly present to Plato's mind. So important, in fact, is the implication of this word, that on its interpretation may depend one's right to be classed as a true Platonist.

As in the philosophical mythology Goodness

is placed at the apex of the Ideas, whence its influence reached down the ladder of life, so in the theological view of creation Goodness is the motive of God's action and the end of being. "He was good," says Timaeus at the beginning of his tale, "and in the good there never can be envy of aught. And being free from this quality, he desired all things to be as like to himself as possible. This is that sovereign principle of creation and of the universe which we most certainly shall be right in accepting from wise men. For God, in his desire that all things should be good and that, so far as possible, there should be nothing evil, took the visible material as it came to him, lying not in a state of rest but moving without harmony or measure; and out of disorder he brought it into order, thinking such a state altogether better than the other." And so, when the act of creation is completed, the world is a place of forms and motions ordered to the end of goodness, in so far as is permitted by *natural necessity* consenting and yielding to the persuasion of reason. 29E

In the use of this word "necessity" as signifying at once the substance of creation and the obstacle in the way of the divine plan, we see how the ethical basis of Plato's philosophy becomes in his cosmogony teleological. Here, as always, his point of departure is the consciousness of our moral being; goodness is purpose, and evil is the hindrance to purpose. And if there may seem to be some taint of the pathetic fallacy in such a reading of human motive into nature, it is fair to remember that any comprehensible theory of the cause of things must incur the same condemnation. The modern conception of natural law, though expressed in the most strictly scientific terms, will in the end be found to depend on an implicit trust in the submission of nature to reason and rightness. The chief difference is that the modern man of science, in formulating his general hypotheses, is likely to be less aware of his mental processes and more subject to naive illusions than was Plato.

But if necessity has this teleological aspect, it has also another aspect in which formal reason rather than moral purpose is pre-eminent. Looked at in one way (which is the essentially Platonic way) the theory of a divine cause and necessity exhibits even the material world as the field of ethical Ideas; from another point of view it seems for the moment to leave these in obscurity, and shows only the rational Ideas of form and number. Then it may be that the immortal soul itself, whether animating the universe as a whole or the individual creatures within the universe, is described in the language of a geometrician, as possessing the faculty of reason and self-government because its secret motions follow the laws of mathematical proportion, and, *a fortiori*, the material world is conceived as a rational system because of the imposition of these same laws upon the chaos of necessity. We are in the realm of physical science.

In accordance with the popular notions of the day Plato divided matter into the four elements; but these were rather variations of one aboriginal substance in its fiery, gaseous, liquid, and solidified states than separate and permanent substances. I shall not attempt to follow his elaborate account of the production of these elements and of their combinations and mutations. In brief, Plato traces geometric forms back to their origin, and finds that the simplest figures are the scalene and the isosceles triangle. By combinations of the former he constructs the equilateral triangle, and from this the three regular solids—the pyramid, the octohedron, and the icosahedron. Out of the isosceles triangle he constructs the square, and from this the cube. By the imposition of these four tridimensional figures on the formless substratum he creates respectively his four elements—fire, air, water, earth. The actual phenomena perceived by us, as well as the organs of perception, result from the adhesions, transmutations, and interactions of these elements caused by the unresting impulse which they bring with them out of the aboriginal flux of necessity.

Many of the details of Plato's system display the faults of a mind too easily satisfied with *a priori* reasoning, yet in its main outlines it is one of the most grandiose and fruitful of human inventions. The substance of the world as he saw it was intrinsically that to which the chemist and physicist of today are looking—a field of energy the differentiations of which are expressed in numerical formulae, or, in other words, a combination of motion and form. The whole reach of manifest existence, from the obscure actions of the atom to the uttermost sweep of the revolving spheres of the heavens, falls into a vast mathematical equation. Much of the inspiration of this theory came to Plato, no doubt, from Pythagorean and other sources, but what to his predecessors had been a vague dream he saw as a coordinate and rational system. So far as the mathematical interpretation of the material universe can be attributed to the invention of one human brain, the honour of the achievement belongs to Plato.

It is not strange that the *Timaeus* should have been one of the most influential of Plato's works. Through the Middle Ages the rôle of the Demiurge harmonized sufficiently with the Hebrew

Jehovah to shape the Christian conceptions of creation, while the Ideas as models of the visible world could be accepted as the eternal thoughts of God, thus bringing philosophy and theology into a peaceful union. With the Renaissance other aspects of the Dialogue came more to the front, and played no inconsiderable part in that mathematical revival which, side by side with the biological and inductive principles of development, marked the great awakening of science. But it must be admitted, however reluctantly, that, so far as the influence of Plato has been felt in this direction, it has tended to foster rather an improper subordination of philosophy to science than a furtherance of legitimate scientific discovery. And for this degradation of philosophy, though it is in essence the very contrary of Platonism, we cannot entirely exonerate Plato himself. It may not be fair to blame him for the common failure to comprehend what has been called his economy of method, his habit, that is, of taking for granted that the main theses of his philosophy will be kept in memory by his reader and need not be constantly repeated when some outlying question is under consideration. Nor is it to his discredit that he was always the searcher after truth, winding his arguments sinuously back and forth in such a way that one not naturally akin to him in spirit may easily miss the steady tidal setting of his thought. But it is a different matter when at times he allows himself to be so far carried away by subordinate interests as to approach something like treachery to his own deeper intuition. In particular there is abundant evidence in the Dialogues and elsewhere that in his old age he wandered into a mathematical mysticism for which enigmatic is a mild word. The numerical proportion on which the soul of the world is constructed in the *Timaeus*, [35A ff] the calculation of the great year of existence in *The Republic*, [546B ff] to take the examples that have maddened innumerable commentators, are fantastic and, at bottom, meaningless. It may be also that in his lectures on the Good he permitted this lust of science to usurp a place in the realm of ethical dialectic which he himself had denied to it. We can in a way understand his purpose and justify his procedure. These mathematical entities to which he reduced moral values were, we may suppose, not actual numbers, but the principles of number—if such a phrase means anything. The quantitative Ideas of unity and division might be taken as symbols of the qualitative Ideas of dialectic; and for this substitution there is a certain intellectual justification, as I have pointed out, so long as the character of the substitution is not forgotten. But such a procedure is at least perilous in itself, and was certainly disastrous in its consequences. It was almost inevitable that his followers, lacking his own sure intuition, should seize on this mathematical symbolism and apply it in the crudest fashion to the expression of dialectical truths—how crude the fashion we may see in the spurious continuation of the *Laws* entitled *Epinomis*. This recrudescence of Pythagorean speculations must have begun very soon after Plato's death. At least we know that Xenocrates, who succeeded Speusippus, Plato's nephew, as head of the Academy, defined the world-soul and individual souls as self-moving number. Naturally the critics of Platonism laid hold of this madness and exaggerated its importance. Aristotle[8] did not hesitate to ridicule the theory of Xenocrates in particular as the most absurd ever broached by man.

This is the phase of Platonism that, despite its early critics, has been cropping up in modern times ever since the Renaissance. It would not be easy to say how far these unexpected results may be traced to a renewed interest in Plato along with the revival of science, and how far they are attributable to the natural inclination of the human mind to magnify the scope of its own achieve-

[8] *De Anima,* I, iv, 16.

ments.[4] But certainly the analogy of the geometrical scheme of the *Timaeus* with the mechanistic hypotheses of Descartes is sufficiently close to suggest at least an unconscious causal relation between the two. And from Descartes the mischievous confusion comes to a climax in Spinoza, who undertakes to interpret the world by an argument proceeding from axioms to theorems and corollaries after the rigorous manner of Euclid's geometry. From such a system teleological design and liberty of the spirit are absolutely excluded. If the universe is to be explained entirely on mathematical principles, it must be purely mechanical in its structure, with no place for spontaneity or deliberate purpose. The Darwinian law of evolution by natural selection, in which biology joined hands with a mathematical law of probability, gave new sanction to the inclusion of the human spirit in the grinding cogs of a huge machine. The "block universe" of Huxley, though he violently repudiated Platonism, is in reality a late stage of the scientific philosophy that, apparently, was imported into the Academy by Xenocrates. And in our own days we have the much-applauded efforts of Mr. Bertrand Russell

[4] For the influence of Platonism and Neoplatonism in this respect, see Kurd Lasswitz, *Geschichte der Atomistik* I, pp. 264-269.

and certain of the so-called New Realists to reduce the Platonic Ideas to mathematical entities.

It is easy, as I have said, to see how this subjection of philosophy to mathematics may be associated with certain unguarded statements of Plato in the *Timaeus* and elsewhere, but it rests, nevertheless, on a total misconception of his real position. The relation of dialectic to science is, in fact, precisely the same in the *Timaeus* as in *The Republic*. The two realms of Ideas at their beginning lie close together, and the knowledge of the one may almost coalesce with the knowledge of the other. At least in the degree of certainty attending them the moral generalizations from our conduct may seem at their start to differ little from the mathematical and geometric abstractions of the intellect; but the progress from the two classes of generalizations is in diametrically opposite directions. In the case of dialectic we proceed from hypothesis to the unhypothetical facts of ethical experience, and so, by the gradual elimination of what is contingent, rise to the immediate consciousness of that element of the soul which is the basis of our moral nature, and to the imaginative conception of God, or the Good, as the primal cause of order and beauty and joy in the world; whereas in the case of science we proceed by continually immersing the Ideas deeper and deeper into the lawless unknowable flux of necessity. As we pass from the pure science of mathematics to the more mixed and complicated fields of physics and chemistry and biology, our laws become continually less rigorous, our formulae more subject to exception and reversal, our generalizations more dependent on the accumulation of detailed observation. It is for this reason that all through the *Timaeus* we find Plato, as soon as he leaves the abstractions of number and form, employing the words "probable" (*eikos*), "probably" (*eikotôs*) ; and the measure of the gap between scientific conjecture and dialectical assurance may be taken by comparing the constant and unabashed use of such phrases in the *Timaeus* with Plato's scorn and contempt in the *Phaedrus* and elsewhere for the sophistical substitution of probability and flattery for the unyielding truth in questions of civic and personal morality. To ascribe knowledge and certainty to physical science and to deny man's inner freedom by imprisoning the spirit in a huge mechanism of fixed and calculable natural law is to invert the whole order of the Platonic philosophy.

The result of such an inversion is shown strikingly in the different connotations of the word "necessity" in Plato and Marcus Aurelius. To the former necessity meant the resistance of the meaningless and incomprehensible flux of things, whether in nature or the human soul, to the government of order and happiness; it was the exact contrary of the spirit, which is shrined in liberty. To the imperial Stoic necessity was the binding force of the whole world, leaving to the spirit this poor relic of freedom alone, that it might form its own opinion as to the moral character of the universal flux of which it was itself also a part, and so might persist in praising that as good which it felt to be evil. The stoicism of a Marcus Aurelius was not without its forcible consolations, but for all its protestations it was intrinsically a doctrine of sadness and of spiritual sterility; and the modern stoicism of science is gray with the same disease. More than that, there is no stable foundation of conduct in this physical necessity taken as a substitute for spiritual law. In the end men will clamour for release from such joyless servitude; if they cannot discover the way of freedom in the law of the spirit, they will throw open the gate of the soul to the throng of invading desires, and the stoical necessity of science, save for the few exceptional minds, will remain as a theory, while in practice the mass of mankind will follow a rebellious and epicurean individualism.

CHAPTER VIII

METAPHYSICS

BY metaphysics I should say that, here and elsewhere, I mean something different from philosophy. The latter is the sincere and humble endeavour to make clear and precise to ourselves the fundamental facts of our conscious life, and than philosophy, as Plato says in the *Timaeus*, no greater good has come nor ever will come to mortal men as a gift from the gods. Its method and its truth are summed up in the three Socratic theses—scepticism, spiritual affirmation, and the paradoxical identification of virtue and knowledge. Metaphysics differs from philosophy in this, that it essays to give a consistent explanation of the *rerum natura,* including our consciousness, in the terms of pure reason, thereby playing false to the law of scepticism and forcing a rational reconciliation upon the Socratic dualism. Reason in itself is the faculty of combining and dividing.[1]

47B

Phaedrus 266B

[1] For this traditional definition of reason see Maximus Tyrius VI, iv a. For the drive towards unity see Plotinus V, iv, 1; for the contrary tendency, Epicurus, *Epist. Prima,* 41.

Thus, in what may be broadly called the world of science, reason is properly employed in combinations ending in mathematical unity and in divisions proceeding to the infinitesimal. It fulfils also a most important function in philosophy, so long as it follows the perception of actual similarities and differences in what may be called the quantitative field of our moral experience; the whole sphere of practical virtue is to this extent dependent upon it. But reason becomes metaphysical—or eristic, as Plato would have said—the moment it presumptuously disregards the dualism of consciousness and attempts by its own naked force to build up a theoretic world of abstract unity excluding multiplicity or of abstract multiplicity excluding unity. Morally expressed, it is equally the error of metaphysics to explain away the reality of evil in favour of some conception of infinite goodness or to deny the existence of the absolute Good in favour of some conception of infinite relativity.[2]

The former error, that of false idealism, crept into the Academy at an early date. From the commentary of Proclus on the passage in the *Timaeus* concerning the goodness of God and God's treatment of the flux of necessity in creation,[3] it ap-

[2] For this distinction between dialectic and eristic (or metaphysic) see *Philebus* 17A.

[3] See the preceding chapter, p. 229.

pears that these words were the battleground of two great schools of interpretation, echoes of whose wrangling still disturb the air of quiet study. The leaders of one of these sects were Plutarch and, more particularly, Atticus (not, of course, the friend of Cicero, but a writer of the second half of the second century A.D.), who saw in Plato first of all the ethical philosopher. To them the distinction between good and evil was primordial and eternal. The substratum of the flux existed always, and received its impulse to chaotic motion from an eternal soul of evil. Here they would have been wiser had they been satisfied with Plato's deliberate choice of the ambiguous word "necessity" for the nature of this substratum, instead of laying undue emphasis on a phrase in the *Laws* and erecting our consciousness of 896E good and evil into an unverifiable hypothesis of two world-souls. A more serious error lay in introducing the order of time into the moral order, and in insisting on a temporal priority of the flux and the soul of evil to the event of creation. To this degree they changed the allegory of the *Timaeus* to a rationalized transaction, and laid themselves open to charges of inconsistency which their opponents were not slow to drive home.

The other school, represented by Porphyry, Iamblichus, and the later Neoplatonists generally, including Proclus himself, sought for the cardinal doctrine of Plato in intellectual Ideas (despite the fact that Plato had subordinated these unmistakably to the ethical order of which alone we have pure knowledge), and so virtually denied the antinomy of good and evil in favour of a rationally unified conception of the universe. Starting with the assumption of a superessential monism, they rebuked the views of their dualistic opponents as impiously abrogating either the goodness or the omnipotence of God. If God, they said, is both absolutely good and creatively omnipotent, then his work of creation must be eternal and entirely good. Brought face to face with the question of existing evil, they explained it away by a vast hocus-pocus of metaphysical emanations and subsumptions. The Whole is absolutely one and absolutely good, but by its very attribute of being it must be productive of other being, and creation becomes a process of endless self-division of the One which somehow leaves the One undivided. The members so produced are good, as related to the whole; they may appear evil, as related to one another. Evil is merely a contingent of subordinate existence[4]—all of which, to the mind hungering after the truth, is nothing but "words, words, words."

[4] *Πᾶν τὸ κακὸν κατὰ παρυπόστασίν ἐστι.*—Proclus, *In Timaeum* 116A.

Now, whatever may have been the mistakes of Atticus otherwise, in his insistence on the prime importance of both good and evil as facts not to be juggled out of sight he was faithful to his master in the matter which really counted philosophically; and, in general, the little we know of him from Proclus and Eusebius leads us to esteem him as one of the few genuine Platonists, and to regret the loss of his works as a calamity. It is, perhaps, the most deplorable event in the history of philosophy that the true tradition of Platonism was swallowed up in Neoplatonism and never to this day has escaped from the verbal metaphysic of a Proclus.[5]

Plato's own attitude towards the claims of

[5] There is an interesting passage in the introduction to Thomas Taylor's translation of the *Select Works of Plotinus*, which shows how the leaders of the romantic revival, by a natural affinity, turned for their Platonism to the Alexandrian interpreters. "For though Crantor, Atticus, Albinus, Galen, and Plutarch," he says, "were men of great genius, and made no common proficiency in philosophic attainments, yet they appear not to have developed the profundity of Plato's conceptions; they withdrew not the veil which covers his secret meaning, like the curtains which guarded the adytum of temples from the profane eye; and they saw not that all behind the veil is luminous, and that there divine spectacles everywhere present themselves to the view. This task was reserved for men who were born indeed in a baser age, but who being allotted a nature similar to their master were the true interpreters of his sublime and mystic speculations. Of these Plotinus was the leader, and to him this philosophy is indebted for its genuine restoration, and for that succession of philosophic heroes [Porphyry, Iamblichus, Proclus, *et al.*], who were luminous links of the golden chain of deity."—And still today the English editor of the *Timaeus*, Mr. Archer-Hind, in his note to the passage under consideration (30A), expressly ranges himself with the Neoplatonists.

metaphysics is best seen in the Dialogue, called by the name of his great monistic predecessor, in which he comes to close grips with the rational contradictions inherent in the doctrine of Ideas; and our view of his philosophy is likely in the end to be coloured by our interpretation of this extraordinary piece of writing. Now it may be admitted at once that, if ever there was a problem that verified the proverb *quot homines tot sententiae,* it is the meaning of the *Parmenides.* The literature on the subject is enormous, and is based on views not only divergent in various degrees but often mutually destructive. I take it that the Platonist or the student of philosophy generally will at least be grateful for a classified survey of these interpretations, however he may feel disposed towards the new interpretation which I have the temerity to add to the list already portentously long.

To begin with the extremists. There are those who see in the Dialogue a frank and unreserved attack on the doctrine of Ideas, and who, accordingly, reject the work as spurious, on the ground, mainly, that Plato himself could not possibly have treated the central thesis of his philosophy in this manner. The first to support this view was Socher.[6] The other extreme is represented by Fouillée, who takes the Dialogue throughout as

[6] *Ueber Platon's Schriften,* published in 1820.

a positive argument *for* Ideas.[7] His position is briefly this: in the first part of the Dialogue Parmenides shows that the union of contraries in the sensible world implies a similar union of contraries in the Ideas, and that the difficulties which concern the participation of sensible things in Ideas will be solved when we see how one Idea participates in another. Hence the second part of the Dialogue takes up this point, and demonstrates that whatever hypothesis you start with, it always involves the primitive union of contraries, the radical union of the one and the many. Thus, whatever pair of Ideas you may consider, positive and negative, you will always find a mediating term in some third Idea, so that all Ideas, even those mutually contradictory, enter into one another and are reconciled in the supreme Unity. In other words, for Plato read Hegel.

To these two extremes should be added Grote's cavalier denial of any consistent meaning at all in Plato. He regards the theory of Ideas supported by Socrates in this Dialogue as genuinely Platonic, and at the same time regards Parmenides' attack on the theory as "most powerful" in itself and as beyond the reach of Plato's answer. The whole Dialogue has no other purpose than to clear the mind of false and hasty assumptions: "It is

[7] *La Philosophie de Platon* I, 203, 204.

certainly well calculated to produce the effect intended—of hampering, perplexing, and putting to shame the affirmative rashness of a novice in philosophy."[8]

Now these interpretations cannot all be right, and I think it would be easy to demonstrate that they are all wrong. As for Socher, it is sufficient to say that the Dialogue bears on every page indubitable signs of the master's hand, and to ask who else could have written it. This intrinsic evidence is so convincing that almost all scholars now accept the work as authentic. Moreover, the objections lose their point as soon as we have found (as I think we shall find) an interpretation which gives the Dialogue an important and integral place in the whole metaphysical discussion of Plato's later years. On the other hand, Fouillée quite overshoots the mark. Virtually to ignore, as he does, the validity of the arguments against Ideas is simply to read the book with closed mind. As for the second part, even Zeller, from whom he borrowed his Hegelianizing method, recognized that the nature of the antinomies here employed indicates an absolute gulf between true Being and the empirical world of time and space.[9]

Grote maintains his position with his usual

[8] *Plato and the Other Companions of Sokrates* II, 295.
[9] *Die Philosophie der Griechen*[3] II, i, 565.

cleverness and honesty, but I doubt if he has any followers today. To hold that Plato never attained a philosophical position of his own, and that the great bulk of his works contains no positive plan or conviction, is to fly in the face of common sense.

Those who take a middle ground between the extremes of Socher and Fouillée are so numerous that it would be intolerably tedious to deal with them individually. We can get the same result more commodiously by a rough classification of the points which, with negligible shades of difference, are variously combined in their theories. On one point they pretty well agree: they nearly all acknowledge the strength of the Parmenidean attack on the position held by Socrates in this Dialogue; they differ in their methods of avoiding the disagreeable consequences of this admission. They all make Parmenides the mouthpiece of Plato in this first part of the Dialogue, but to some of them the "young" Socrates is vainly attempting to support an embryonic theory of Ideas which Plato had now outgrown, whereas to others Socrates is arguing for a theory of Ideas (as entities separate from the world of phenomena) which was advanced by enemies of Plato, whether frankly as their own or in Plato's name, or was erroneously supposed to be Plato's by inconsiderate pupils of the Academy. By exploding this false doctrine Plato, either directly or inferentially, is enforcing the genuine doctrine of Ideas as pure conceptions of the mind, or as "the basis of potentiality," or "scientific laws," or "the methodic foundation of experience." In other words, they differ in naming the source and degree of the error supported by Socrates, but they all agree in holding that, in one way or another, the Dialogue looks to a rationalizing *reconciliation* of the difficulties inherent in the doctrine of Ideas; they all, in various ways, belong to the metaphysical school represented of old by Proclus and in modern times by Hegel.

Now the first difficulty in these explanations is the supposition that in a question vital to his whole philosophy Plato would have chosen Socrates as the mouthpiece of the doctrine he wished to combat. The difficulty is not quite so overwhelming, I admit, if we assume that the "young" Socrates is arguing for a genuine Platonism now outgrown rather than for a pseudo-Platonism. But such an assumption throws us into another insurmountable difficulty. No doubt in the course of his growth Plato changed somewhat in his attitude towards Ideas; it could hardly be otherwise. But there is nothing in his writings to indicate such a complete break as must be assumed by this explanation of the *Parmenides,* whereas, on the contrary, there are passages in his latest works which speak strongly for the essential continuity of his philosophy in this respect.

Timaeus 28A
Laws 965C

Against those who would see in Socrates the champion of pseudo-Platonism, there are two further objections. On the one hand the conceptualist doctrine of Ideas which they regard as genuinely Platonic is clearly embraced among the various explanations set up by Socrates and knocked down by Parmenides. On the other hand, in this very Dialogue it is shown that the rejection of Ideas as existing apart in a sphere above our own involves the rejection also of the divine government and knowledge of the world—a conclusion so abhorrent to Plato that he could not have accepted the premise. And I hold it demonstrable (though to prove the point would require a separate essay) that the whole recent movement to deprive Platonic Ideas of some sort of independent reality for the imagination is, on the bare face of it, a perversion of the simple facts, for the conscious or unconscious purpose of confirming the tendency of present-day thought by the authority of a revered name of the past.

Parmenides 132B

Ibid. 134D

When they come to the second part of the Dialogue these mediators take different and contradictory grounds. Some of them hold that

Parmenides remains the spokesman for Plato throughout, and that, having exploded the false doctrine of Ideas, he now demonstrates the true doctrine. To these the same reply must be made as was made to Fouillée: this second part of the Dialogue, unless violently distorted, is, like the first, negative from beginning to end, and to discover in it a positive exposition of any doctrine is a forced reading of what is not written. Others hold that Plato first used Parmenides as his own mouthpiece to destroy the pseudo-doctrine foisted upon him by the Eleatics, and then, in a superrefined spirit of revenge, turns the tables by making Parmenides exhibit the fallacies of his own Eleatic philosophy of the one. This explanation contains, as we shall see, a half truth, but it overreaches itself in taking Parmenides now as the exponent of Platonic truth and then as the exponent of Eleatic untruth. Plato was subtle enough, in all conscience, but he was not quite so disconcertingly double-faced as that. And, further, though a minor result of the second discussion may be to expose the untenability of the Eleatic unity in its absolute, exclusive form, the primary intention and achievement of Parmenides will turn out to be of an entirely different nature.

So much for the interpretations which run counter to common sense or to plain statements in the Dialogue itself or to the whole tenor of Plato's philosophy. A few scholars have partly or wholly avoided these errors, and have left explanations which are rather inadequate than false. Among these is the author of the *Greek Thinkers*, with whom, considering his general attitude towards Greek philosophy, I find myself rather unwillingly yoked. Gomperz holds that the *Parmenides* was written at a time when Plato's mind was in a state of fermentation. Attacks from the Megarians, or new Eleatics, had united with his own deepened reflection to disturb him with difficulties in regard to the very basis of his metaphysical theory of Ideas. He could not at this time answer these difficulties, neither could he surrender his whole philosophy. In his zeal for the truth, therefore, he brings together all the arguments against Ideas, making no discrimination between those that are answerable and those that are not. In this way he delivers himself, so to speak, and is free to pass on. He piles up all sorts of arguments against the metaphysical school from which had proceeded the sharpest attacks on the theory of Ideas. After the date of the *Parmenides* we see two things happening: Plato's searching analysis of hostile doctrines brings out by way of indirect proof the inevitability of the doctrine of Ideas, and the trial through which he has passed leads him to modify his own principles.[10]

One thing is thus seen by Gomperz which ought to be clear to any one who reads the Dialogue with open mind: the logic against Ideas is conducted with relentless rigour, and is not directed against a particular form of the doctrine but against all its forms, including conceptualism.[11]

But another thing is clear. Plato did not for a moment admit that this logic, however rigorously conducted, rendered the doctrine of Ideas in itself untenable. As we have seen, he continued to ad-

10 *Griechische Denker* II, 437-440. In many respects my theory of the *Parmenides* agrees also with that expressed by Professor Shorey in his *Unity of Plato's Thought.*

11 132B: "Perhaps," says Socrates, "each of these Ideas is only an act of cognition, and is nowhere present except in the mind." Only in one place does Parmenides leave the position of Socrates unassailed. Socrates proposes a simile by which he thinks that possibly the indivisible integrity of the Idea may be reconciled with its presence in the multiplicity of objects which partake of its nature: "Just as day, being one and the same, is simultaneously present in many places yet is not separate from itself [that is, does not lose its integrity by being among the events of time], so each Idea might be in all things yet remain one and the same" (131B). Instead of replying to this argument, Parmenides shifts the comparison to a tent spread over a number of men; in which case not the whole tent but only a portion of it should properly be said to be over each man. Did Plato himself fail to see that by shifting the simile from time to place he was leaving the real point untouched, or did he perceive the difficulty of determining the nature of time itself, whether it has any objective reality, and so shrink from a discussion which would have been out of all proportion to the scope of the Dialogue? All the difficulties raised by Parmenides involve the conception of Ideas as *in space.* Can a metaphysical psychology avoid this fallacy?

here to the doctrine in his later works, and, more than that, this very Dialogue contains direct statements of his adherence. The strongest of these is in the words of Parmenides himself, where, at the close of the discussion which has driven Socrates 135B point by point to a complete silence, he asks what is to be done about philosophy if we surrender our belief in Ideas, or whither we shall turn our minds, or, indeed, how we shall be able to converse at all.

Such a passage ought to be sufficient in itself to refute those who find in the *Parmenides* any surrender of the distinctly Platonic doctrine of Ideas, but its force and emphasis are doubled when we remember that it does not stand alone, but is a repetition of—rather a brief reference to—Plato's constant argument against the anti-idealists of the Heraclitean and Protagorean school. This point is important enough in itself and in its bearing on the place of the *Parmenides* in the whole drift of Plato's metaphysical period to warrant us in pausing a moment to consider such a passage as the close of the *Cratylus*. The bulk of this Dialogue is given up to a series of linguistic puzzles which have been one of the bugbears of Platonic students. Many of the derivations suggested by Plato are so absurdly extravagant as to force the conclusion that he was ridiculing the pretensions of certain etymologists of the age;

yet others, again, seem to be advanced quite soberly by him, and the reader is left with no criterion to distinguish between satire and serious exposition. This bewildering medley of fun and earnestness is not absent in other Dialogues; is indeed one of the marks of the Platonic method. But whatever Plato's attitude may have been towards the legitimacy or illegitimacy of the current etymological science of the day, he seems to have felt that the Heraclitean notion of the flux was natural to the unreflecting mass of men and was deeply imbedded in the elementary substance of language. Any seeker for the truth, therefore, must free his mind from the implications of common speech and train himself to look at things as they are. The fact is, says Socrates at the close of his discussion with the "young" Cratylus, that those who gave this colour to language did so, not because our world is a huge perpetual flux, but because their own minds were revolving dizzily in a sort of whirl, into which they had fallen and are dragging us after them. The only escape for us is not to consider individual objects which may be good or beautiful, and the like, and which appear to us to be continually changing, but to fix our minds on Ideas, such as the good itself, the beautiful itself. For how can we even give a name to a thing which is now this and now that, always

439c ff

altering and slipping away from us at the very moment we are speaking of it? There is no knowledge of such a thing; for just when you are going to know it, off it goes into something else, so that you have no chance to learn what it is or what qualities it has. There isn't any knowledge—nothing to be known and no one to know, if all things are in this state of unceasing flux. Granted the faculty of knowledge in us, then there must be something for it to know; then there must be those Ideas of goodness itself and beauty itself, and the like, which do not belong to the cosmic stream and whirl. It may be hard to decide between the truth of these Ideas and what the Heracliteans and Protagoreans and all the rest of them believe, but certainly he is a pretty poor creature who will permit the life of his soul to be determined by the mere implications of common speech, and will ignorantly assert that there is nothing sound in the universe but that the whole thing is a sort of leaky vessel continually at drip. How would he differ from a man who was suffering from a rheum, and was convinced accordingly that the whole world was in a state of rheumy fluxion? You at least, Cratylus, are still young, and ought not to accept these current theories out of hand, but should investigate them bravely and honestly.

Now there can be no doubt that the brief exhortation to the "young" Socrates was written in the same tone and to the same general end as that to the "young" Cratylus. The interpretation of the *Parmenides* thus depends on the solution of this crux: we have the whole doctrine of Ideas subjected to a process of destructive logic to which Plato makes no direct answer either here or anywhere else in his writings, and by the side of this we have an unwavering statement of the reality and vital importance of Ideas. Given this dilemma the only way of escape would seem to be through holding that Ideas do not come to us by a process of metaphysical logic, but by means of some direct experience independent of such logic, and that the method of reasoning employed against them by Parmenides, while perfectly sound in itself, is all *in vacuo*, so to speak, and has no bearing upon their existence or non-existence. No other interpretation would appear to be tenable, and as a matter of fact the second, and larger, part of the Dialogue is directed to exhibiting the limitations, and the usefulness within these limitations, of what I have called the process of metaphysical logic. To understand this point we must look a little more closely into the antecedents and structure of the Dialogue.

Parmenides, the principal speaker of the Dialogue which bears his name, was the pre-Socratic philosopher from whom more than from any other, unless it be Pythagoras, Plato's thoughts received their colour. His name sounded to Plato out of antiquity with peculiar awfulness, and even when disagreeing with him the younger man could not forget his veneration. Against all the other philosophers, from Homer down, who had seen in the world only the play of flux and perpetual mutation, Parmenides stood forth in lonely grandeur, a man, in the Homeric phrase, "reverend and dreadful," a sage able to impress Socrates with "the noble depth of his mind." In Elea of Magna Graecia he had set up a school in direct opposition—so it seemed at least to Plato and the later men—to that of Heraclitus. In his cosmic poem he represents himself as carried by the Sun-maidens up to the Gate of Night and Day, which is opened to him by the goddess Dikê (Right, Justice), and there in the realm of heavenly light he is instructed in the difference between truth and deceptive opinion. The whole vision was to be taken over by Plato in *The Republic* when searching for the nature of justice, and worked up into his sublime comparison of the supreme good in the moral sphere with the light-giving sun in the physical sky. And the truth as Parmenides saw it was one aspect, incomplete and therefore partly false, of what Plato was to hold. Our opinion of

Theaetetus 183E

the world of change and appearance is a mere deception; rather, such a world *is not,* for the reality of being is the reality of thought, or knowledge, one and indivisible, without beginning or end, without growth or decay, finite in itself and with nothing beyond it, with no colour or motion or quality of perception. The universe of Parmenides was the pantheism of his predecessor Xenophanes, but as it would be expressed by an intuitive philosopher instead of a religious dreamer.

Now it was inevitable that this one-sided perception, or intuition, of the unity underlying all things should have been met with ridicule on the part of those who could see nothing but the world of flux, and it became necessary for the Eleatic pupils of Parmenides to support their master by means of whatever logical instrument they could lay hands on. The shrewdest of these defenders was Zeno, who sought to discomfit the enemy by bringing confusion into their own camp. The Heracliteans had undertaken to dispose of the Eleatic unity by showing the absurdity of a theory which, by its maintenance of indivisibility, involved the denial of our common perceptions of motion and change, and by its insistence on absolute uniformity, involved the denial of all qualities to things, thus reducing the mind to a state of complete negation. Zeno did not, indeed could not, answer these criticisms directly, but he did undertake to strengthen the Parmenidean position by setting forth the equal absurdities that followed if we rejected unity and made multiplicity the essence of all things. One of his arguments was the famous riddle of Achilles and the tortoise. Suppose Achilles, who runs ten times faster than the tortoise, tries to catch a tortoise that has a start of ten feet. By the time he has traversed these ten feet, the tortoise will be one foot in advance. When he has traversed this foot, the tortoise will be a tenth of a foot in advance; and so on *ad infinitum*. That is to say, on the assumption that time and space are divisible this division will proceed without end, and Achilles never can overtake the tortoise; which is absurd on the face of it. Another argument of Zeno's turned on the contradictions that must arise from the ascription of qualities to things. For instance, if you say that A is like B, this will imply that A is unlike something else, so that you are driven to the paradox of holding that A is at the same time like and unlike; which, again, is absurd.

All this, of course, might be waived aside as an amusing play of logomachy, but in fact it introduced a real evil into the life of a people who were already prone by nature to lose themselves in linguistic subtleties and to prize sheer cleverness above simple veracity. Instead of throwing up the whole game the Heracliteans answered Zeno in kind, while on the other hand the Megarian school of Euclides took up the cudgels for the Eleatics and carried their logic to the extreme of fatuity. Hence arose that art of eristic which threatened for a while to reduce the whole of Greek philosophy to a vain babble of contentious words. The very essence of eristic, it will be seen, lies in the metaphysical use of reason, or logic, without regard for, or in flat contradiction to, the facts of experience and intuition. By the time of Plato's maturity these successors of the sophists were expending their strength in ever vainer and more perplexing enigmas, while of the sincere aspiration after the truth it might be said,

> Naked and poor thou goest, Philosophy!

The wrangle had spread until it embraced Plato's own doctrine of Ideas, which hitherto he had held rather as a matter of intuition and as an unquestioned necessity of the imagination than as a reasoned conviction, and was forcing him in self-defence into what may be called his metaphysical period.

One of his aims at this time, perhaps his chief aim, was to expose the vanity of the new form of sophistry—for it was at bottom precisely the same spirit as that which he had opposed in his earlier Dialogues, but disguised now in the sober garb of metaphysics—and in its place to establish the true dialectic, that is to say the generalizing ascent of the reason without losing from sight, indeed by using as its firm stepping-stones, those innate perceptions of moral and aesthetic consequences which he had hypostatized as Ideas. Already, in 454A *The Republic,* he had expressed his scorn of those who, by reason of their inability to distinguish Ideas, gave themselves up to the pursuit of verbal oppositions, thinking they were practising dialectic, or the true philosophical discourse, when in fact they were indulging in mere eristic. In his systematic exposition of this evil, the first task would be to bring into the light the lurking absurdities of the Heraclitean metaphysic of the flux; this he had done in the *Cratylus, Euthydemus,* and *Theaetetus* with a drastic power in comparison with which the campaign of Zeno and the other Eleatics was mere child's play. Now, in the *Parmenides,* he would employ the same weapon, only with greater respect for the persons concerned, against the Eleatics and Megarians, and at the same time would investigate the validity and scope of the whole metaphysical, eristic method.

For this purpose he took advantage of the occasion when the aged Parmenides had visited Athens with his pupil Zeno, and had there met and talked with Socrates, then a "very young man." There are, I know, difficulties in the way of accepting this meeting as historical, but Plato mentions it so often, and in such a manner, that we are almost bound to regard it not only as a fact but as one to which Socrates was fond of alluding. That, however, is unessential. Whether as a fact or fiction, we are told in the *Parmenides* that Zeno has been reading those treatises of his in which, as I have said, he undertook to support the Parmenidean unity by showing that the multiplicity assumed in its place by the Heracliteans led to even greater paradoxes. Socrates listens attentively, grasps the point of the argument, but has a modest question to ask. I see, he says, that material phenomena are at the same time both one and many; for instance I, as I stand here, am one if I am taken as a separate integral member of this group of men, but I am many if you consider me as composed of parts, right and left, upper and lower. I can understand how your logic by laying hold of these contraries will reduce our reason to a paradoxical *impasse*. That seems easy enough if you start with material phenomena. But I should like to hear how you would apply this process to Ideas. What, exclaims Parmenides, with concealed pleasure, wishing to bring out his clever young questioner, do you believe in these Ideas as real things having an existence apart from phenomena? Whereupon follows the famous attack on the doctrine, which turns on the difficulty of comprehending how an Idea can be immanent in the many particular phenomena which bear its name without losing its integral unity, or how phenomena can participate in the Idea without forgoing their character of changing multiplicity. Socrates is completely blocked in all his efforts to explain away this difficulty—indeed neither Plato nor any one else has ever found a positive solution of the paradox—and is ready to throw up his position as untenable; when Parmenides checks him. No, says the old warrior, you cannot do that, for without Ideas you are confronted by a still more disastrous paradox; unless these generalizations of the mind correspond to things in some way really existent there can be no philosophy, no knowledge, no meaning at all in conversation. You yourself have declared that the logic of Zeno did not touch the simple fact of experience which presents phenomena to us as at the same time both one and many, and you need only carry the method out to its legitimate end to discover that it will leave you in possession also of your intuitive belief in the parallel existence of Ideas and phenomena. Then, after some hesitation, Parmenides is persuaded to give an illustration of this self-denying use of eristic. Now it should be observed here that this interpretation of the first part of the Dialogue—in itself the only one which does not do violence to the plain sense of the text—avoids the absurdity of supposing that Plato would have selected Socrates for the spokesman of a theory he meant to denounce. To represent Socrates, when "very young," as not yet competent to maintain his position with the full mastery of dialectic is quite another matter, and is in perfect conformity with Plato's own transition, not from one philosophy to another, but from what may be called his purely intuitional period to the years of metaphysical examination into his creed.

As for Parmenides' eristical exhibition, which forms the second part of the Dialogue, it is just one of the terrible things of philosophy; heaven forbid that I should ask my reader "to swim through such and so great a sea of words." But without a glance at the main points of the discussion we cannot assure ourselves of the general purport of this Dialogue or understand the drift of the Dialogues that follow.

Parmenides 137A

Parmenides, then, condescends to submit his

own doctrine of the One as a *corpus vile* to be tried out by his eristical method. He will first take the statement that the One is and trace the consequences, and will afterwards deal in the same way with the contrary statement that the One is not. The argument thus drags its awful length through these eight hypotheses (I alter their order as noted):

A (This stands first in the Dialogue): The One is posited as absolute and indivisible. It follows from this hypothesis that the One is devoid of all qualities, incapable of being known or in any way considered or named or uttered.

B (Second in the Dialogue): But by the very hypothesis that the One *is* we attribute being to it. Thus the One is presented as a duality of unity and being; this duality is subject to further division, and the One becomes endlessly divisible and possessed of infinite qualities. But to say that it possesses every possible pair of contrary qualities is the same as to say that it has no qualities; and we are reduced to a similar absurdity.

Now let us consider the consequences of this hypothesis for the Many (*ta alla*, that is, the Others, all things conceivable besides the One):

C (Fourth in the Dialogue): If the Many are taken as having no participation in the One, *i.e.*, as absolute multiplicity, it follows that, like the

One of A, they will have no qualities at all, and are utterly inconceivable.

D (Third in the Dialogue): If the Many participate in the One, then, like the One of B, they will have all contrary qualities, which is equally repugnant to reason.

So far we have been arguing on the supposition that the One is; now let us take the contrary supposition that the One is not:

E (Sixth in the Dialogue): If the One is not, regarded absolutely, we get the same total negation as in A.

F (Fifth in the Dialogue): But by the very hypothesis that the One *is* not we associate being with it. To say that the One is not is a different thing from saying that the Not-One is not, and in this way altereity, the property of difference, is brought into the Not-One, and the Not-One (like the One in hypothesis B) becomes possessed of all different qualities. (This hypothesis, it should be noted, is in metaphysical form the old thesis which Plato had wrestled with in earlier Dialogues and was to discuss at length in the *Sophist,* that there is no such thing as a false statement, for the reason that it is impossible to speak what is not.)

G (Eighth in the Dialogue): If we take the One as not being absolutely, it follows that the Many will have no qualities at all and there is nothing.

H (Seventh in the Dialogue): If the One is

not but the Many are, it follows that, by seeming to be composed of units, the Many will have all contrary qualities.

Now, there are two ways of looking at these hypotheses. According to most of the interpreters one set (A, C, E, G) is meant to show the impossibility of positing an absolute One apart from the Many, whereas another set (B, D, F, H) demonstrates the reconciliation of the One and the Many. Thus hypothesis A leads to a total negation, whereas hypothesis B, by reconciling the One and the Many, leads to the possibility of predication and corresponds with actual experience. The whole argument, in a word, is a continuation of the assault on the doctrine of Ideas as entities of real existence apart from phenomena (*chôrista*), and a proof that, by some theory of conceptualism or the like, they are in and of the Many.

The other way of interpreting the argument is to accept all the hypotheses as resulting equally in an *impasse,* since it is just as absurd to say that a thesis leads to the simultaneous possession of all contrary qualities as to say that it leads to the total negation of qualities. And this in my judgement, as my wording of the summaries above will have made evident, is the only interpretation the language of Plato will bear. Of course, if you care to do violence to the text, you may get any meaning out of it you choose; and that capable scholars are not above using violence can be shown from a shining example. After deducing from the second hypothesis the possibility of attributing all qualities to the One, Plato adds a corollary in which, by a subtle analysis of the time element, he shows how this is the same as saying that the One would have no qualities. Very good. But how does Professor Burnet in his summary of the hypotheses deal with this double-edged argument? He states the conclusion of the hypothesis proper thus:

"Therefore One partakes of past, present, and future; it was, it is, it will be; it has become, is becoming, and will become. It can be the object of knowledge, judgement, and sensation; it can be named and spoken of."[12]

That is as close to the Greek as need be; but turn now to his statement of the conclusion of the corollary:

"It is the instantaneous which makes all changes from one opposite to another possible, and it is in the instant of change that what changes has neither the one nor the other of its opposite qualities."[13]

[12] *Greek Philosophy,* Part I, p. 268.
[13] *Ibid.*

Compare this with the actual conclusion, which is literally as follows:

"By the same token it [the One], passing from one to many and from many to one, is neither one nor many, is neither divided nor combined. And, passing from like to unlike and from unlike to like, it is neither like nor unlike, neither made like nor made unlike; and, passing from small to large and to equal and to the opposites, it would be neither small nor large nor equal, neither increased nor diminished nor made equal."

Is it too much to say that, by transposing this conclusion from a negative to a positive form, Burnet has come pretty close to betraying his author? The case is still worse with a critic like Natorp, who out of an argument ending thus in complete negation draws a positive meaning such as this:

"By the instrumentality of continuity, as we may now put it briefly, the way is prepared for a reconciliation between the absolute position (the thesis) and the relative (the antithesis). The possibility is opened for the passage of the absolute position into relativity, that is to say, for the passage of the Idea, first conceived as pure thought, the *a priori,* into experience, which means the realm of relativity. The first foundation is laid for the possibility of experience as methodically assured knowledge."[14]

[14] *Plato's Ideenlehre,* p. 256.

There is not a hint of all this in Plato; it is Kant or Hegel or Natorp. The conclusions of the second hypothesis and of its corollary ought to be enough in themselves to show that no such inference can be drawn. But to clinch the fact, the whole Dialogue ends sharply with this formidable summary: "Thus, it seems, whether One is or is not, both it and the Many, regarded both in themselves and in relation to each other, all in every way both are and are not, both have appearance and have not." How a scholar can have this consummation before his eyes and yet fail to see that all the eight hypotheses must be taken without distinction as reductions to the absurd, is beyond my comprehension.

Certain owlish persons who are aware of this consequence have worried themselves over the method by which it was obtained. It is full of fallacies and false reasoning, exclaims Apelt,[15] and will waive the whole thing as a piece of youthful indiscretion. Fallacies, quotha! It is indeed an arsenal of fallacies; rather, it is the fundamental fallacy of metaphysics from the beginning until now, stripped of its garb of irrelevant truths and laid bare to the gaze of any who will see. For I take it that any metaphysic which attempts to

15 "Wahres Arsenal von Erschleichungen und Sophismen," *Beiträge*, p. 32.

give an account of the ultimate nature of things, the *rerum natura,* by the process of pure reason will impale itself on one or the other horn of this dilemma: either it will cling honestly to the absolute One or the absolute Many, and so move about in the void, with no content of meaning; or it will surreptitiously merge the absolute One in the concrete one or the absolute Many in the concrete many, and so fall into a dishonest mixture, or "reconciliation," of contraries. This is not the place to support such a charge by detailed illustrations, but I think it would not be hard to show how perfectly the error of Spinoza's system is exposed by Plato's second hypothesis (B). Compare with the working out of that hypothesis Spinoza's effort to deduce all the contrary qualities of phenomenal existence from the absolute One: "Transeo iam ad ea explicanda, quae ex Dei sive entis aeterni et infiniti essentia necessario debuerunt sequi: non quidem omnia (infinita enim infinitis modis ex ipsa debere sequi)."[16] In like manner the scientific conception of a "block universe," as an absolute closed system, falls under the third hypothesis (D), or, in the Spencerian form of the Unknowable and the Knowable, under the fourth hypothesis (C). On the other side, the various forms of Pragmatism, all the systems that

[16] *Ethics* II, Praef.

accept only the absolute flux, including the much-bruited metaphysic of M. Bergson, will come within the scope of one or another of the four hypotheses that assume the One as not being.

I would not insist on this modern application; but at least I do not see how the second part of the Dialogue can be understood otherwise than as an endeavour to deal in such a manner with the metaphysic, or eristic, which had sprung up by the side of true philosophy in Plato's own day. And the results obtained are of a double nature. The first four of the hypotheses discover the embarrassment into which those of the Megarian school were driven who, in fanatical opposition to Platonic Ideas and the Heraclitean flux, ran to an uncompromising idealism of the One, as the exclusive reality. I do not believe that Plato meant to direct his argument against the Parmenidean unity itself (cf. 128A); that unity, as the Idea of the Good, was so deeply imbedded in his own teleological philosophy that it is impossible to think of him as trying to eradicate it. Rather, his aim must have been to tear away from this unity the scaffolding which had been raised about it by the later Eleatics and Megarians, and so to leave it in the form of an obscure intuition, such as it appeared to Parmenides himself, untouched by the rationalism which would petrify it into a logical negation of experience. Even so, it is notable that Plato treats this error with a certain respect; at least his exposition is conducted without any admixture of that contemptuous buffoonery which he had employed in the *Euthydemus,* when "dusting the jackets" of the two shameless Protagoreans. He was himself a spiritual child of the ancient sage, and thought it almost an act of parricide to lay hands on "father Parmenides." In this way we can understand the propriety of making Parmenides the instrument of attack on his Megarian successors.

Sophist 241D

But this freeing of the Parmenidean unity from its eristical supergrowth was by the way, so to speak; the main intention was to bring relief to Plato's own doctrine of Ideas. At the conclusion of the first part of the Dialogue we found ourselves confronted by this dilemma: one by one the arguments set up to explain the relation between Ideas and phenomena had been knocked down, yet it was declared impossible to surrender Ideas. The situation was very much like that taken by Dr. Johnson (the great Socratic of the modern world) in regard to a question of equal ethical importance: "All theory is against the freedom of the will, all experience for it." By demonstrating that the eristical method led to the same absurdity (and so destroyed itself) whether we posited the One as existing or as not existing, Parmenides would intimate to his young friend that to guard himself against a rationalism which brought out the contradictions involved in positing the existence of Ideas he should have retorted by forcing his antagonist to admit the contradictions involved in positing the non-existence of Ideas. Thus he would have made himself free to accept the reality of Ideas as a necessity of inner experience, just as he had seen that the eristic of Zeno and the Heracliteans left him free to accept the reality of phenomena as known to perception.

This interpretation of the *Parmenides,* I submit, avoids the violences to the text to which other interpretations are bound to have recourse. It justifies the choice of speakers, and does away with the arbitrary assumption of a radical break in Plato's philosophy. It has also the advantage of finding a single purpose running through the two parts of the discussion, and of establishing an integral relation between this Dialogue and the others in which Plato turned his attention from the sophistry of rhetoric to the sophistry of metaphysic.

If any further confirmation of this thesis is needed, it may be found in the natural interpretation of a much-disputed passage of the Dialogue which is commonly, and rightly, I think, regarded as supplementary to the *Parmenides*. In the central part of the *Sophist* Plato considers 242cff in turn three classes of philosophers. First, by an argument essentially the same as that employed in the *Parmenides,* he reduces the Eleatics and Megarians to confusion. He next deals with the opposite school, not the mere Heracliteans in this case, but the gross materialists who cling to brute sensations and wage war upon the idealists of all 246A colours, a veritable *gigantomachia*. These, or their kindred at least, he had already made the subject of biting ridicule; now he is content with what is really little more than a reference to the proofs he has elsewhere given at length. He argues briefly 247B that there is a soul, or life-giving principle in us; that there is a difference between the just and the unjust soul; that this difference is due to the possession and presence of justice or its contrary in the soul, and that, therefore, justice itself exists as an invisible, impalpable entity—that is to say as an Idea. After dismissing these two opposed 248A sects, he turns to the "friends of Ideas"; and here the interpreters run amuck. Campbell, in his note, thus states the various positions held:

"Four possible suppositions remain, if we believe the dialogues to be the work of Plato. The 'friends of forms' are either (1) Megarians (since Schleiermacher this has been the most general impression); or (2) Plato himself at an earlier stage; or (3) Platonists who have imperfectly understood Plato. The fourth hypothesis combines (2) and (3)."

Now, in the name of conscience, why should not an unsophisticated reader take these friends of forms, or Ideas, to be just Plato and his true followers, without any beating about the bush?[17] In the first place, as we have seen above, Plato, in his contention against the materialists, assumes the existence of Ideas in precisely the manner[18] of his early Dialogues. The *Sophist,* therefore, can scarcely contain a rejection of Ideas, or any radical change in the way of regarding them. What follows? Plato subjects these idealists to the antinomies of reason, thus (I borrow Campbell's own summary):

"Perfect Being [the realm of Ideas] cannot be in a state of mere negative repose, a sacred form without thought, or life, or soul, or motion. . . . But on the other hand, thought is equally impossible without a principle of permanence and rest. Hence the philosopher, with whom thought is the

[17] Some colour may be lent to Campbell's third supposition by the words of 248c (*πρὸς δὴ ταῦτα κ.τ.λ.*). They may, in fact, point to the overzealousness of Platonists (or of Plato himself in his unguarded moments) who held the definition of Ideas too rigidly; but the statement of 248A (*καὶ σώματι κ.τ.λ.*) is so perfectly in accord with Plato's position in the *Timaeus* and elsewhere as to leave room for no doubts of the nature of these "friends of Ideas." It is to be noted that the exposition of the theory comes from the mouth of an Eleatic.

[18] Ἕξει καὶ παρουσίᾳ.

highest being, can listen wholly neither to the advocates of rest nor of motion, but must say with the children, that 'both are best,' when he is defining the nature of Being."

We have, then, in this section of the *Sophist* an exact repetition in brief of the method employed in the second part of the *Parmenides,* applied now directly to the doctrine of Ideas. And observe that the conclusion is in no sense of the word a "reconciliation" of rest and motion, the One and the Many, nor is it in any sense a determination of the relationship of Ideas to phenomena, but a categorical statement that Ideas are and that in some unknown way they show the effects of their power in the realm of multiplicity and change. The destruction of eristic and metaphysical assumption by means of an unwavering affirmation of the reality of moral Ideas, united with an unwavering scepticism, is Plato's philosophical justification of his master's life and faith.

But candour forbids us to stop here. Though this is the significant outcome of Plato's later thought, it is clear that, for a while at least, he was haunted by the hope of attaining to some discursive proof of those Ideas the existence of which could only not be disproved by the false methods of eristic, and to some rational explanation of the inherence of these Ideas in phenomena. There are

tentative efforts to create this positive metaphysic in the *Sophist* and the *Philebus,* but it should appear that the full working out of the plan was left for the projected Dialogue on the *Philosopher.* Sophist 253c
The absence of that work from the Platonic canon means, I conjecture, simply this, that Plato became aware of his inability to achieve what, indeed, no philosopher has ever achieved; since it lies beyond the scope of human reason.

CHAPTER IX

CONCLUSION

GRANTED that Platonism has been expounded correctly in the foregoing chapters, the question remains—a very grave question—whether its influence has been on the whole for good or for evil. The extent of this influence no one, I think, will deny. As a dominant factor in the formation of the Christian religion it has helped to mould the civilization of the western world, and as a philosophy in its own right it has been the inspiration of innumerable poets and prophets who have called upon men to rise above ephemeral interests to the contemplation of all time and all being. In a manner not given to any other writer Plato must be regarded as the liberator of the spirit, who has set wings to the human soul and sent it voyaging through the empyrean. But in that flight how many have mounted too near the sun, and fallen to earth in ruinous combustion! How many others have forever lost their way in those thin heights! Alas,

Republic 486A

for the weakness of mankind, and their "blind hopes"! It is a fact, sad and indisputable, that no one is more likely to call himself, or to be called by his admirers, a Platonist than the reformer with a futile scheme for the regeneration of the world, or the dreamer who has spurned the realities of human nature for some illusion of easy perfection, or the romantic visionary who has set the spontaneity of fancy above the rational imagination, or the "fair soul" who has withdrawn from the conflict of life into the indulgence of a morbid introspection, or the votary of faith as a law abrogating the sterner law of works and retribution. Half the enthusiasts and inspired maniacs of society have shielded themselves under the aegis of the great Athenian. Not to mention the detected mountebanks, the list is replete with the names of accepted sages whose wisdom, if brought to the test, would prove to be only a finer form of spiritual flattery.

If these are the only products of Platonism then it is a pity the works of Plato were not lost altogether, with the books of so many other ancient philosophers, and we who busy ourselves with interpreting the Dialogues are merely adding to the sum of the world's folly. But it is not so. It is with Platonism as with Christianity and every other strong excitement of the human heart.

Liberty is the noblest and at the same time the most perilous possession that can be given to mankind; and, unless we are prepared to silence the higher call of religion and philosophy altogether for the safer demands of a purely practical wisdom, we must expect, while we try to expose, these vagaries of minds made drunk with excess of enthusiasm. No, we dare not repudiate Platonism for the dangers that surround it; but it is well that we should be put on our guard against Platonists, remembering the admonition of St. John to the disciples of Christ: "Believe not every spirit, but try the spirits whether they are of God, because many false prophets are gone out into the world."

We have already had occasion to distinguish between the true and the false Platonist in the realms of art and science; but there is need of a single general criterion which can be applied to every pretender to the name, and such a criterion, happily, is not far to seek. Both the true and the false Platonist appear with the promise of regeneration in their hands, stimulating the imagination to roam in unbounded and unfamiliar fields, loosing the soul from the prison-house of convention, pointing to a prize beyond the rewards of commonplace prudence. But there is this certain difference between them. To the true Platonist the divine spirit, though it may be called, and is, the hidden source of beauty and order and joy, yet always, when it speaks directly in the human breast, makes itself heard as an inhibition; like the guide of Socrates, it never in its own proper voice commands to do, but only to refrain. Whereas to the pseudo-Platonist it appears as a positive inspiration, saying yes to his desires and emotions. Goethe unwittingly was giving expression to the everlasting formula of pseudo-Platonism when he put into the mouth of Mephistopheles the fateful words: "I am the spirit that ever denies." It is God that denies, not Satan. The moment these terms are reversed, what is reverenced as the spirit becomes a snare instead of a monitor: liberty is turned into license, a glamour of sanctity is thrown over the desires of the heart, the humility of doubt goes out of the mind, the will to follow this or that impulsion is invested with divine authority, there is an utter confusion of the higher and the lower elements of our nature.

This longing for the assurance of faith without the humbling bondage of scepticism extends, of course, far beyond the sphere of pseudo-Platonism, and has been the ever-present temptation of those strong men, of whatever professed creed, who have laid violent hands on religion and philosophy. Here is the origin of those enthusiasms and extravagances of inner freedom which are constantly rising to trouble the world by making an unholy divorce between supposed inspiration and common sense, sometimes between supposed inspiration and common morality. The manifestations of fanaticism may be various, in accordance with the disposition of the man or group of men upon whom the temptation falls, but the ultimate cause is always the same: it is the lust of the heart to identify our personal inclinations with the voice of God or with some divine authority. In religion this spirit is seen at work in the pride of the ascetic —"the hair shirt, the watchings, the midnight prayers, the obmutescence, the gloom and mortification of religious orders, and of those who aspired to religious perfection," as Paley says.[1] For the ascetic is simply the man who translates the inhibitions of the spirit into a positive law of physical discomfort. From the same source came the lust of persecution into the Catholic church, leading a man like Torquemada to believe that his passion for dominance was the divine will; and the equal intolerance and inhumanity of the Puritans, who, as was charged by the writer of a tract in 1676, held that "the Holy Spirit directs and persuades men what to believe and do [note the affirmation] by his immediate working." It was

[1] *Evidences* II, ii, 2.

not without reason that South could say they fetched "a warrant for all their villainies from ecstasy and inspiration." There was needed the whole revulsion of the eighteenth century to "cast enthusiasm out of divinity," to use Bishop Sprat's strong phrase—the pity being that so much of the true inspiration had to be ejected with the false. Turn again to Paley, the apostle of common sense in religion, if not of common sense at the expense of religion, and hear his measured rebuke of the wild language of the sectarian who cherishes the emotions attendant upon so-called "conversion" and "rebirth" as evidences of sanctification: "Our Saviour uttered no impassioned devotion. There was no heat in his piety, or in the language in which he expressed it; no vehement or rapturous ejaculations, no violent urgency, in his prayers. . . . I feel a respect for Methodists, because I believe that there is to be found amongst them much sincere piety, and availing, though not always well-informed, Christianity: yet I never attended a meeting of theirs, but I came away with the reflection, how different what I heard was from what I read! I do not mean in doctrine, with which at present I have no concern, but in manner; how different from the calmness, the sobriety, the good sense, and I may add, the strength and authority, of our Lord's discourses!"[2]

Nor has the evil been less marked in philosophy than in religion, as he who writes in this time of universal war can testify with sad conviction. There is a saying of Kant's which is much quoted: "Act on a maxim which thou canst will to be law universal"; it is the formula of his so-called categorical imperative. Well, no one would hold Kant directly responsible for the calamity to civilization wrought by the European War; the causes are manifold and complicated. Yet, after all, what is the ambition of Kant's people but this maxim in actual operation? For the moment you identify the moral sense with the human *will,* as Kant did, and bestow upon this will a certainty and authority above the negations of pure reason, you are in imminent danger, however you may hedge yourself about with precautions, of confounding your law universal with the *libido dominandi* and of seeing in the categorical imperative an excuse for forcing your own sense of right upon reluctant mankind. One cannot follow the course of German thought from Luther through Kant and Fichte and Hegel, through Mommsen and Treitschke and others who have justified the aggression of their national statecraft, without a growing conviction that the boasted idealism of

[2] Evidences II, ii. 3.

the Teutonic mind, if not of the Northern mind generally, has been vitiated from the first by an inability to hold the will to refrain (if we may so name the daemonic check without ourselves suffering the ambiguous consequences of the word "will") distinct from the will to power.[3]

These are examples of the evil that fastens upon the better part of the soul whenever men are tempted to identify spirituality with their positive will. The danger of the seduction, whether for religion or philosophy, was pointed out by Hooker clearly enough in his contention with the Puritanic temper of his day. "For my purpose herein is to show," he said, "that, when the minds of men are once erroneously persuaded that it is the will

[3] Paulsen, in his famous commentary, is continually alluding to the "Platonism" of Kant, yet unwittingly, in passage after passage, shows how far Kant's rationalistic (and utterly inconsistent) dualism is from the ethical dualism of Plato, and how easily it slips into a dogmatism of the will. "With immediate certainty," he says, "we affirm moral good as the real purpose of life. We do this, not by means of the understanding or scientific thinking, but through the will, or, as Kant says, the practical reason. In the fact that the will, which alone judges things as 'good' or 'bad,' determines morality as that which has absolute worth, we have the point of departure for the interpretation of life." The result of this he states elsewhere: "Perhaps we may say that there is an inner relationship between Kant's ethics and the Prussian nature. The conception of life as service, a disposition to order everything according to rule, a certain disbelief in human nature, and a kind of lack of the natural fulness of life, are traits common to both. It is a highly estimable type of human character which here meets us, but not a lovable one. It has something cold and severe about it that might well degenerate into external performance of duty, and hard doctrinaire morality." (*Immanuel Kant,* by Friedrich Paulsen, translated by J. E. Creighton and Albert Lefevre, pp. 5 and 54.)

of God to have those things done which they fancy, their opinions are as thorns in their sides, never suffering them to take rest till they have brought their speculations into practice. The lets and impediments of which practice their restless desire and study to remove leadeth them every day forth by the hand into other more dangerous opinions, sometimes quite and clean contrary to their first pretended meanings: so as what will grow out of such errors as go masked under the cloak of divine authority, impossible it is that ever the wit of man should imagine, till time have brought forth the fruits of them: for which cause it behoveth wisdom to fear the sequels thereof, even beyond all apparent cause of fear."[4] But long before Hooker's day the matter was set right by Plato, once for all, in the conversation between Socrates and Euthyphro, the profoundest and most beautiful, I sometimes think, as well as the most perfectly Socratic of the Dialogues. There the fanaticism of a young man who has no hesitation in holding his own extravagant notion of holy procedure as identical with the absolute law of holiness is contrasted with the ironical modesty of Socrates, now an old man full of experience, who, never doubting the reality of the Idea of holiness as an eternal peremptory fact, yet knows that the transference of the Idea

[4] *Ecclesiastical Polity,* Preface, viii, 2.

into the region of specific action can be only tentative and subject to correction. Those who have understood the *Euthyphro* need read no further to learn the true relation between the spiritual affirmation of Socrates and Plato and their scepticism.

Fanaticism, as I have said, is rather contrary to Platonism than pseudo-Platonic, and is by no means confined to those who pretend to be followers of the Academy. The perversion of those who falsely assume Plato's name more commonly takes the guise of an idealism in which the softer emotions of the soul masquerade as the spirit. In this form pseudo-Platonism is almost synonymous with the romantic movement which has carried and still carries with it so many of the finer minds of the age. For us romanticism seems to have begun with the revolt from the narrow restrictions of neo-classical authority in the eighteenth century, but its roots really go back to the theosophic speculations of Alexandria. There its chief exponent was Plotinus, who took up the ancient metaphysical error of Parmenides, and sought to re-establish the doctrine of an all-embracing unity in place of the irrational dualism of the master in whose name he pretended to teach. From this unity—to summarize the perplexed inconsistencies of Neoplatonism in the briefest terms—the creation of the world was supposed to proceed by a series of emanations, through intelligence and soul, down to body, or material "necessity," which, as the last and remotest offshoot of the divine, was converted somehow, in a manner never cleared by Plotinus of the obscurity inherent in any monistic system, into the cause of evil. This "necessity" of the Plotinian metaphysic may seem to have some resemblance to Plato's substratum of the same name, but the difference is really fundamental. With Plotinus the final "necessity" is not so much an independent inexplicable force, of which the divine government is a negation, as it is a vaguely conceived distance from the divine, a "deprivation" (*sterêsis*), so to speak. Though at times Plotinus falls into the common language of the Stoics and sees a shadowy sort of evil in the existence of individual souls as a breaking up of the supreme unity, at other times he admits a view of the world which virtually juggles evil out of it altogether. "God made me," he says, speaking for the universe, "and I am come from him, perfectly fashioned out of all living beings, sufficing and sufficient unto myself, in want of nothing." In such a scheme the individual acts in accordance with the necessity of his nature: "each man also does what comes natural to him, and different men do different things." Plotinus was not unaware of the deductions that would be drawn from such a doctrine: "By saying that there is no evil at all in the universe, we perforce do away with the good as well, and deny that there is any desirable end to be attained." In such a conclusion of nihilism Plotinus was unwilling to rest, and he twists and struggles to escape the net of his own logic; but if he escapes at all, it is only into a kind of etherialized naturalism. Let us grant that the great Neoplatonist was filled with cravings for truth; his doctrine of emanation and necessity and *sterêsis,* none the less, by weakening the sense of evil as a positive force, and by identifying salvation with a surrender of the soul to vague yearnings for completion, is one of the sources of the endless stream of pseudo-Platonism.[5]

First in the list of the modern pseudo-prophets, the father of all the brood, is Rousseau, who, in the words of his latest expositor, "with modifications due to the influence of Montesquieu," remained "essentially a Platonist to the end."[6] Now, to discover the essential creed of Rousseau one need not look far. It is stated explicitly in a famous

[5] The quotations here used are taken from *The Problem of Evil in Plotinus,* by B. A. G. Fuller. To that study I would refer those who desire to look more thoroughly into a subject of great moment which I have been obliged to treat in the most summary fashion.

[6] C. E. Vaughan, *The Political Writings of Jean Jacques Rousseau* I, 236.

passage of the *Nouvelle Héloïse*: "Only the souls of fire know how to combat and conquer; all the great achievements, all the sublime actions, are their work; cold reason never has accomplished anything illustrious, and we triumph over our passions only by opposing one to another. When the passion of virtue arises in the soul, it dominates alone and holds all in equilibrium." There is, no doubt, a half-truth in such words, as there is in all pseudo-Platonism. Without the heart, without deep feeling and strong desires, it is true that no great work is achieved whether for good or for evil; that is the express doctrine of *The Republic*. But to look for balance in the mere opposition of passion to passion, to make morality only one passion among many, is to preach a ruinous perversion of Platonism. "As for Julie," Rousseau says, "who had no rule but her heart, and knew no other more sure, she abandoned herself to it without scruple, and to do well needed only to do what it demanded of her." The philosophy of abandonment is not Plato's. It may be that of Goethe, the romantic, who, having made Mephistopheles the spirit of denial, could put no better word for God into the mouth of Faust than feeling (*Gefühl*), and could discover no better use for that feeling than the seduction of an innocent girl.

491A ff

In England we shall find another leader of

romanticism who is revered by many today as a Platonist and as an emancipator of the human spirit. The message of Blake is elusively uttered, but simple enough in itself. It is fairly well summed up in his two mythical personifications of good and evil, "Emanation" and the "Spectre," who play their parts in *Milton* and other of his Prophetic Books. What little Blake knew of the Alexandrian philosophers came to him at second hand from Jacob Boehme, but his principle of goodness is clearly nothing more than a personification of that instinct of self-expansion in the superessential One which Plotinus made the cause of the unfolding universe. The Emanations, according to Blake, come forth "like Females of sweet beauty"; they are the power of the imagination, the perfect spontaneity of desire, the innocence of unquestioning impulse. Against them in each man is set his evil Spectre, which is nothing else but the man's own shadow regarded as the questioning, limiting, restraining reason:

> They take the Two Contraries which are
> call'd Qualities, with which
> Every substance is clothèd; they name
> them Good and Evil.
> From them they make an Abstract,
> which is a Negation
> Not only of the Substance from which
> it is derivèd,

A murderer of its own Body, but also a
murderer
Of every Divine Member. It is the
Reasoning Power,
An Abstract objecting power, that
negatives everything.
This is the Spectre of Man, the Holy
Reasoning Power,
And in its Holiness is closèd the
Abomination of Desolation![7]

There could not be a more extraordinary amalgamation of abstract reason as a process of cold logic, such as it had become in the school of the rationalists and pseudo-classicists, with reason as the spiritual inhibition which Socrates worshipped in the daemonic check, and both forms of reason Blake rejects as the spectral abomination. "Jesus," he declares, "was all virtue, and acted from impulse not from rules."

Those who care to see the mythology of Blake developed in splendid imagery and chains of long-drawn sophistry may take up the works of Shelley, the purest of the English romantics—a Platonist also, as most of his admirers will have him. "Under forms of thought derived from the atheist and materialist Godwin," we read in one of the best informed of living British critics, "Shelley has given, in *Prometheus Unbound,*

[7] *Jerusalem* f. 10, ll. 8-16.

magnificent expression to the faith of Plato and of Christ."[8]—The faith of Plato and of Christ! Shall I confess that to meet with such words in such a place is to be overborne with the futility of writing at all. What shall a Platonist say? what shall he not say? The most casual student ought to perceive that the *êthos* of Shelley's drama, through its superficial paraphernalia of classic and Platonic borrowings, is antipodal to true classicism and Platonism. If words mean anything the poem breathes the spirit of rebellion against the idea of the divine as a restricting, inhibiting power and is animated by the dream of deifying the emancipated emotions in its place. Here, if anywhere, the voice that denies is evil:

> Music is in the sea and air,
> Wingèd clouds soar here and there,
> Dark with the rain new buds are dreaming of:
> 'T is love, all love!

(Love, the unconvinced reader must add, which does not exclude hatred and bitter intolerance of those who have worshipped a different God.)

These pseudo-Platonists you shall know, then, by a single test: they all grasp at the imaginative and emotional elements of Platonism, but forget that the spiritual affirmation speaks from a dark

[8] C. H. Herford, *Cambridge History of English Literature* XII, 74.

recess of the soul (dark, Plato would say, from excess of light), in which no image of mortal likeness is seen, and into which no positive motive can enter. And so you shall find them substituting untrammelled spontaneity for centralized control, endless expansiveness for obedience to the inner check, and an exaggerated sense of personal importance for the impersonality of the spirit. They are the sons of Plotinus and citizens of Alexandria.

But if the last word of Platonism viewed from the personal side of reason and concupiscence, as the last word of all genuine spirituality, is a negation, we are not, therefore, to suppose that it signifies or commands an impoverishment of our human existence. The very contrary of that is true. I would not deny that the dualism of body and soul, which Plato apparently took over from the old Orphic mysteries, led him at times to magnify a pure asceticism, and it is easy to see why this aspect of his teaching exercised a disproportionate influence in those after ages when the world seemed to be breaking up before men's eyes and lapsing into its original chaos. Indeed, remembering the catalogue of ills, such as "to behold desert a beggar born," which drove Shakespeare, the least ascetic of poets, to cry out for restful death, and reckoning up the inevitable treacheries of hope and the feeble results of endeavour, the sullen antipathies or the light-hearted indifference of mankind to all that summons them out of their ephemeral concerns—reflecting on these things, I should not dare to deny that one of the just and permanent offices of philosophy is to create for the anxious soul a refuge from the world. There are times in our day, as there were in Plato's, when no other safety or comfort seems open to us than the way of flight. I would not repudiate the great passage of *The Republic* in which Plato sums up the obstacles confronting any one who, living the philosophic life, would aim to be both in the world and of the world:

"Then, Adeimantus, I said, the worthy disciples of philosophy will be but a small remnant: perchance some noble and well-educated person, detained by exile in her service, who in the absence of corrupting influences remains devoted to her; or some lofty soul born in a mean city, the politics of which he contemns and neglects; and there may be a gifted few who leave the arts, which they justly despise, and come to her;—or peradventure there are some who are restrained by our friend Theages' bridle; for everything in the life of Theages conspired to divert him from philosophy; but ill-health kept him away from politics. My own case of the internal sign is hardly worth mentioning, for rarely, if ever, has such a monitor been given to any other man. Those who belong 496A to this small class have tasted how sweet and blessed a possession philosophy is, and have also seen enough of the madness of the multitude; and they know that no politician is honest, nor is there any champion of justice at whose side they may fight and be saved. Such a one may be compared to a man who has fallen among wild beasts—he will not join in the wickedness of his fellows, but neither is he able singly to resist all their fierce natures, and therefore seeing that he would be of no use to the State or to his friends, and reflecting that he would have to throw away his life without doing any good either to himself or others, he holds his peace, and goes his own way. He is like one who, in the storm of dust and sleet which the driving wind hurries along, retires under the shelter of a wall; and seeing the rest of mankind full of wickedness, he is content, if only he can live his own life and be pure from evil or unrighteousness, and depart in peace and good-will, with bright hopes." (Jowett's translation.)

These are the moments when, looking out on the futility of all things human, we say that the great pilot himself, having dropped the helm from his hands, has retired apart into his watchtower and left the world to be rolled backwards in its course by its own fated and innate desire. Such moments of dejection will come to every thinking man, and for these too philosophy has its healing mission. And when the hour of parting is at hand and the

Politicus 272E

work of life is accomplished, as on that day in the Athenian gaol when Socrates was talking for the last time with his friends and disciples, then, also, philosophy will appear as a study of death and a long preparation for surrender of the concerns of this earth.

But that is not the characteristic note of Plato, nor the aspect of philosophy on which it is well to gaze overmuch. Rather, we should dwell on the fulness of existence that belongs by right to him who has overcome himself. No one, I think, can read the Dialogues without being impressed above all by the broad sanity of the life they inculcate and display. It would require a whole book to exhibit this truth in detail, but some notion of its scope can be obtained by taking a few sentences from a Dialogue in which, from the nature of the subject, one would least expect to meet with these practical uses of philosophy. If, caught by the occasional note of asceticism, any one believes that Plato's teaching is contrary to the maxim of a sound mind in a sound body, he need not study the book of *The Republic* which deals at length with physical training as a preparation for the higher education, but may find the doctrine stated with sufficient explicitness in a few passing words of the *Timaeus*. "All that is good is fair," it is 87c there said, "and the fair cannot be lacking in proportion." Hence the sound man will not suffer his intelligence to grow at the expense of his physical strength—"the soul must not be exercised to the neglect of the body, nor the body to the neglect of the soul, in order that, being a match for each other, they may attain balance and health." That is the foundation, but beyond this the whole tenor of the Dialogue is a witness to Plato's interest in the play of the intellect for its own sake. Particularly in the large observations of natural law he sees a field of endless and elevated activity; 59c "for," he says, "if we pursue these as a source of recreation, not forgetting the principle of eternal being but gaining from the plausible theories of phenomena a pleasure free of remorse, we may create for ourselves a sober and intelligent entertainment for life."

Nor does the concern of the philosopher end with the exercise of the body and the understanding; the arts, too, will be included in his purview, and his will be the genuine love of beauty. 88c Whether his interest is in mathematics, or in any other intellectual pursuit, he will, if he is rightly to be called a cultivated man, apply himself to the 80B arts—not, indeed, as do the common run of the thoughtless, who seek for pleasure only in lovely forms or in the concourse of sweet sounds, but after the manner of those wiser men who find happiness from the imitation of the divine harmony in mortal motions. Thus, as Plato says elsewhere, philosophy is reason tempered by music, the best guardian and saviour of the soul, which alone, if it be born in a man, is able to preserve him in virtue to the end.

Republic 549B

Yet there is also in these studies a higher aim than the immediate gratification and safety they offer. Does any one suppose that he shall reach up forthright to the assurance of spiritual intuition, without the discipline which comes from exerting the brain in the lower sphere of knowledge, or that his eyes shall see God before they have learned to look with sympathetic interest upon the ordered expanse of creation, or that he shall taste the mystery of eternity when he has never cared to acquire the long lessons of time? Possibly for some men this brief and unlaborious path to the summit may lie open; but they will not find it indicated in Plato.

Philosophy, as Plato expounded it in the groves of the Academy, was thus the fulness of life, moving ever to higher and richer planes of knowledge and feeling. Yet it was a life, also, conditioned by the moral law, consciously present as an inner check setting limits to the grasp of reason, staying the flow of desires, governing the imagination, bringing not stagnation and death, as some foolishly suppose, but offering the true liberty wherein alone is the fruition of our nature, and opposing that license whose end is the faction and disease of the soul. The operation of this check, the manner in which the Spirit of God moves upon the face of the waters, we cannot explain; it is of the very essence of dualism that the relation between the elements of our being cannot be stated in positive terms. The beginning and end of philosophy are contained in the spiritual affirmation that it is better to be just than unjust, better to suffer all things for righteousness' sake than to do unrighteousness; but in the daily practice of life no absolute law of just dealing has been vouchsafed to man, and he is left to the stern necessity of approaching wisdom humbly by the slow accumulations of experience, and of learning by suffering. It should appear that Plato, in the proposed Dialogue on the *Philosopher,* had in mind to answer the perplexities of the dualistic paradox once for all, and to set forth the law of the spirit in the language of positive metaphysics. That dialogue he never wrote, in honesty to himself could not write; and who shall presume to supply what the master's hand left undone?

The unfinished window in Aladdin's tower
Unfinished must remain.

But Plato has done for us better than his promise. If the picture of the philosopher as an abstract ideal was not drawn, he has left us in the character and lineaments of Socrates an immortal portrait of philosophy incarnate in a living historic man. I shall not attempt to retell a story the beauty of which lies open for any one to read in its perfection. It is sufficient to point to the lesson of that life as a practical reconciliation of the paradox that baffles reason and drives so many troubled minds to the positive extreme of religious asceticism or to the negative extreme of hedonism. Socrates was no ascetic; I doubt if any citizen of Athens more keenly enjoyed the common pleasures of the day, or was more heartily welcome amongst men of all shades of belief and all modes of living—except among the shams and pretenders. Yet, withal, he walked always with his ear inclined to the voice of the divine inhibition; and when the voice spoke, it was as if an invisible wall was thrown about him, shutting him off from the solicitations of the world. It is not only that he could mingle innocent indulgence with unflinching self-restraint and combine acceptance of the chances of fortune with the clearest self-direction, but there was about him a reserve, a mark of power, a sign of emancipation, which proved that he had bargained with life on his own terms. Those who came close to him knew that what all the world desired, yet threw away, he had.

For, however we may calculate the sum of pleasures and pains in such an existence as that of Socrates, the records, if words have any meaning, leave us in no uncertainty as to his happiness. At the end of the account of his last day in gaol the reporter of the scene declares that to his friends he seemed in death the best and wisest and most just of all men they had known. To these epithets the reporter might well have added "the happiest." That, indeed, is the strongest and most enduring impression we get of the man, his peculiar testimony to the reality of the spirit and to the value of philosophy—his happiness. Other saints and sages have pointed the way to a life in faith, have charmed us by the sweetness of their resignation, incited us by the fires of their charity, heartened us by their great courage, humiliated us by their superiority to temptation, allured us by the vision of heaven upon their faces, taught us, in a measure, the difference between the peace and the pleasure of the soul: but were it not for Socrates, the world, our western world at least, would have no assurance of the supreme victory of the truth in happiness. Herein he was greater than his greatest pupil. With all Plato's sweep of

Phaedo 118

imagination and depth of insight, despite the fact that only through his sympathy and subtle understanding are the master's lineaments really known to us, there are signs here and there in his works that he himself never altogether conquered the world or rose quite above the mists of spiritual pride. I do not mean, in these closing words, to belittle the achievement of one whose writings are the purest source of philosophy yet given to mankind; but it is true, nevertheless, that, though Plato could perceive and depict the serenity of Socrates, he could not completely possess it. And when, in his searching of many questions, he went astray into doubtful paths, as now and then he did, leaving the door open to the strange misconceptions and confusions of a pseudo-Platonism, it was because for the moment he allowed himself to become unfaithful to the humility of spirit which was as much the strength of Socrates as was his certainty of spiritual conviction.

There is a quaint story in Diogenes Laertius which tells how Socrates once met Xenophon in a narrow lane, and, putting his staff across it so as to prevent the young man's passage, asked him where the various necessities of life were for sale. And when Xenophon had answered, he asked again where men might be made good and virtuous. And, receiving no reply, he said, "Follow me, then, and learn." So, as we read the Dialogues of Plato, the figure of Socrates seems to rise before us, challenging us with his queries, and bidding us follow him in the pursuit of truth and goodness. He would not say, if he were to meet us now, that we should make his life in ancient Athens the exact model of our conduct, for that was determined by the ephemeral circumstances of the hour; he would rather command us to deal honestly with ourselves and others, as he had done, and to look for our reward in that happiness which is the crown of philosophy.

THE END

APPENDIX

For the beginner in Platonism the order of reading the Dialogues is of the first importance. The effect of plunging through Plato's works as they are arranged in any of the existing editions or translations known to me is likely to be a state of bewilderment as to what all the talk is about. The traditional arrangement by tetralogies (groups of four) is arbitrary; unrelated Dialogues are there forced together by some purely accidental resemblance, while others, closely related in subject, may be widely separated. On the other hand none of the modern rearrangements is, in my judgement, quite satisfactory. Now, two principles of sequence are open to us, the chronological and the logical; but neither of them is without difficulties. The chronological order in itself no doubt would be the most natural, if only we had some infallible criterion as to the relative time of composition. It is true that certain large outlines of sequence by this canon have been pretty generally agreed on, but the details are still disputed and are not likely ever to be settled. We are thus thrown upon the logical order of ideas; but here again there are serious difficulties. Plato did not always finish one subject and then pass on to another; on the contrary his themes often cross one another in such a way that in a pair of Dialogues one theme may be more developed in what thus seems to be the later of the two in logical order, while the treatment of another theme would indicate that this Dialogue was the earlier. Our only recourse, therefore, is a compromise, and in the arrangement that follows I have proceeded frankly on that principle. In the main the groups there formed would appear to follow one another in the time of composition, as they do, largely considered, in the logical order of ideas; but it is probable that in some cases a Dialogue included in a later group, for instance the biographical, was written before some one of an earlier, let us say, the Socratic, group. Within the groups the arrangement is logical and probably also, for the most part, chronological, though here again it was necessary to compromise. I can only say that the scheme is the one that seems to me to give the clearest general notion of the development of his philosophy. The analyses which follow the diagram are, patently, of the most meagre sort. They make no pretension even to indicate the large subsidiary questions, often in themselves profoundly interesting, which branch out from the main ethical thread of Plato's thought.

SUGGESTED ORDER OF READING

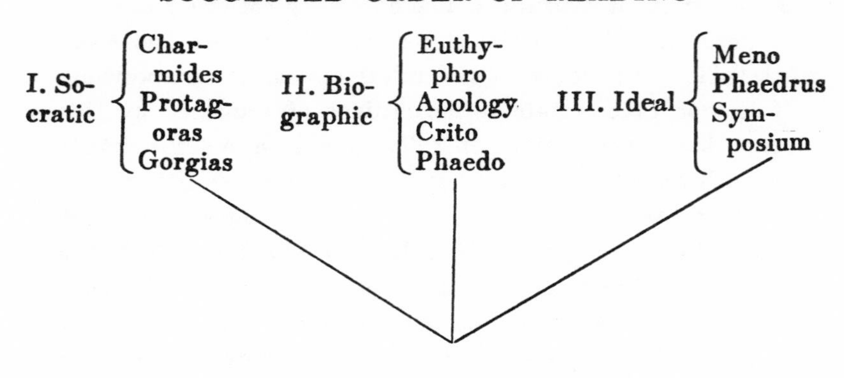

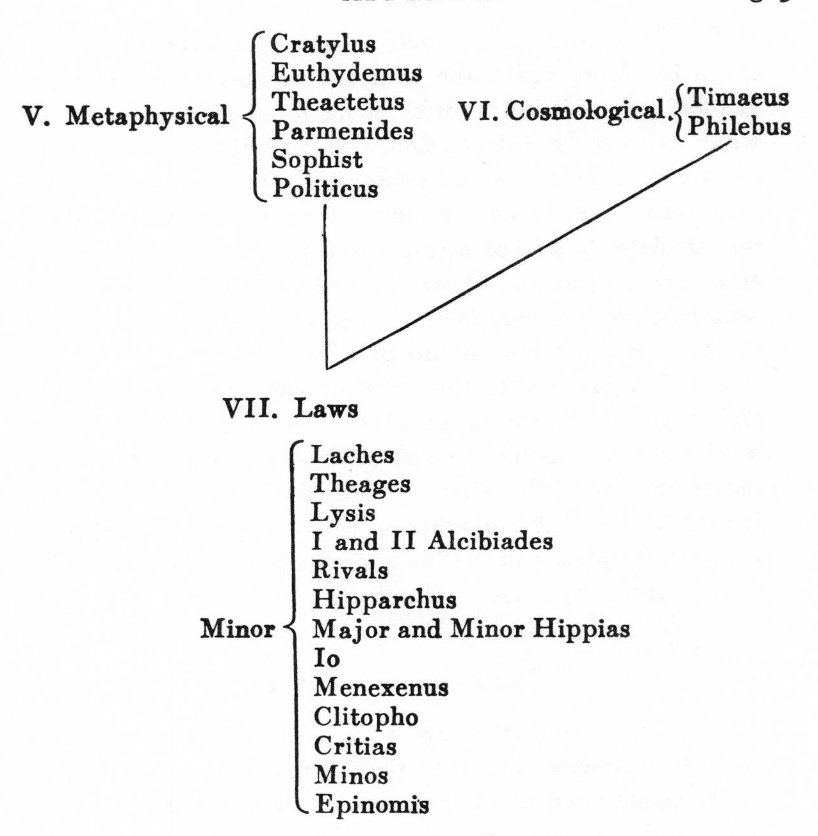

The Socratic Group

In general these Dialogues are aporetic, that is, they set forth the difficulties and bearing of a question without coming to a definite conclusion.

The *Charmides* deals with the nature of temperance. No satisfactory definition is discovered, but we are left with the suggestion that somehow the virtues run together into one and are connected with some form of knowledge.

The *Protagoras* asks whether virtue can be taught like the arts. Thus again the question is raised whether the virtues are all identical with some form of knowledge. In what seems to be a digression, but is really the main point of progress from the *Charmides*, Socrates suggests that virtue may depend on a science of measurement, by which we calculate the sum of pleasure and pain resulting from any act. According to this theory of hedonism the virtuous man would be he who can foresee most clearly the future, and the criterion of virtue would be pleasure.

The *Gorgias* proves that pleasure and pain do not furnish a sufficient law of morality, and takes refuge in the intuition that justice (which now appears as the moral sense, or sum of the virtues) is better for a man than injustice. It hints at a distinction between pleasure and happiness, but appeals to the judgement after death to set right the apparent injustice of this life.

The Biographic Group

These four Dialogues are connected with the trial and death of Socrates. Together they give a portrait of him at the consummation of his life as the philosopher *par excellence*, and are thus a concrete practical presentation of the intuition reached in the earlier group.

The *Euthyphro* presents Socrates, at the eve of his trial, talking with a young friend on the nature of holiness. Euthyphro has no doubt of his perfect knowledge of this virtue as a practical conformity with the will of the gods. Socrates, who is about to defend himself against the charge of impiety, does not question the reality of holiness as an eternal Idea to be sought for and obeyed, but brings out the difficulty of determining what in any case is the will of the gods. To know this we must first know what holiness is.

The *Apology* sets forth the divine mission of Socrates as one called to lead his people to consider the needs of the soul before those of the body. The spiritual affirmation is connected with scepticism, and the probability of an adjustment of the wrongs of life in a future world is still maintained.

The *Crito* shows Socrates in gaol, unjustly condemned to death, yet unwilling to evade human laws by bribing his way to liberty. The belief is expressed that obedience to these decrees of the State will prepare a man to face the judgement of the Divine Laws.

The *Phaedo* shows Socrates dying for his conviction in happiness. He is happy because his real life here and now is already in the eternal immutable world of Ideas.

The Ideal Group

What is this world of Ideas in which the philosopher lives?

The *Meno* resumes the old question whether virtue is a form of knowledge which can be imparted by instruction. It connects Ideas with the things of eternity by the argument of reminiscence. Our knowledge of them, and our impulse to virtue, is a memory of our vision of absolute justice and goodness in some former existence.

The *Phaedrus* places Ideas in a mythical supercelestial sphere, as the *Meno* regarded them in a mythical time. The argument looks forward also to the metaphysical problem of truth and falsehood.

The *Symposium* brings Ideas into life as an ethical force by exhibiting the love and desire they excite in the soul by the attraction of their beauty.

The Republic

Here the arguments of the earlier groups are developed and woven together into a single cord. Justice is the moral sense, and the other virtues are the specific applications of it. The just man, as he is just, has his reward in happiness now and here, and to that extent there is no need to appeal to future rewards and punishments. Justice and happiness are the effect of the Idea of the Good as the supreme cause. The philosopher is he whose life is governed by this cause. The knowledge of ourselves as happy in justice is an immediate certain intuition (the spiritual affirmation), above the practical knowledge, or opinion, which, working in the sphere of the specific virtues, is always subject to confirmation by the future. The constitution of the ideal State is expounded as a counterpart of the perfect philosopher. At the end of the Dialogue the religious sanctions of divine Providence are added to the deductions of philosophy.

The Metaphysical Group

As *The Republic* was the focus of the earlier discussions, so from it radiate the later questions. The earlier contention had been with the rhetorical sophists who, as a class, ignored the authority of the moral law as having any stability apart from the universal flux. Now the ground shifts to the question of knowledge itself; passing from the naïve to the metaphysical doubts of sophistry. The *Theaetetus, Sophist,* and *Politicus* are internally connected, and almost certainly follow in this order. The *Cratylus* and *Euthydemus* are probably earlier, possibly a good deal earlier. The *Parmenides,* logically considered, seems to me to fall best between the *Theaetetus* and the *Sophist*; but there are undeniable objections to this arrangement.

The *Cratylus* plays with the absurdities involved in the popular notion of the universal flux as betrayed by the etymologies of language, and proves the inadequacy of such a criterion for any one earnestly in search of the truth.

The *Euthydemus* makes sport of the thesis that there is no distinction between knowledge and opinion, truth and falsehood. It eliminates this thesis by a reduction to the absurd.

The *Theaetetus* debates the question, What is knowledge? Protagoras had argued that knowledge is obtained only by perception, that there is therefore no distinction between kinds of knowledge, and that the sensations of the individual are the only measure of truth. Socrates rebuts these theses, but comes to no satisfactory conclusion as to the nature of knowledge, that is of knowledge as a relation between subject and object. But he also strongly reaffirms the spiritual fact that we know it is best for a man to live in the world of Ideas, and to imitate in his conduct, so far as this is possible, the justice of the divine nature.

The *Parmenides* first acknowledges the difficulties inherent in any rational explanation of the doctrine of Ideas (and of the moral certainty dependent on this doctrine). Secondly, it affirms the necessity of maintaining this doctrine, and exhibits the inadequacy of the metaphysical use of reason to prove or disprove what we possess by the higher intuition.

The *Sophist* now shows the proper use of the reason, controlled by the content of experience, when dealing with the questions raised by the metaphysical logician. First it arrives at a physical definition of the sophist; then passes to his character; then discusses the nature of being and not-being (the relative), and sets down the sophist as one who deals with the realm of not-being. Meanwhile the second argument of the *Parmenides,* the necessity of maintaining the doctrine of Ideas as an intuition superior to metaphysics, has been restated in summarized form. Ethically the *Sophist* shows connexions with the *Gorgias.*

The *Politicus* undertakes to discuss the character of the statesman on the same level as the discussion of the sophist. Its most interesting part is the long mythical digression on the forward and backward revolutions of the world as it is now guided by the divine will and now left to move by its own innate impulsion.

The Cosmological Group

The exact chronological place of these two Dialogues is problematic. Logically they may be taken as a sequel and development of the mythical digression of the *Politicus.*

The *Timaeus* turns from metaphysics to cosmogony. The dualism of knowledge and opinion has been fortified against the attacks of sophist and eristic; the universe is now shown to present itself to us in a corresponding dualism of the Divine and Necessity. To the former belong ethical Ideas; science ranges in a region between the two. The essential parts of the first account of creation will be found in sections 27D to 31B, 34A to 35B, 36D to 38C, 39E and 40A, 41A to 43C; of the second account in sections 47E to 52D, 69A to 70B, 70DE.

The *Philebus* returns to the old question of pleasure and pain, but with the results of the metaphysical inquiry as a background. Which is the higher, pleasure or knowledge, and what is their relative position in the universal scheme? In answering this question the nature of things is divided into the cause, the limit, the limited, and the limitless; the cause being equivalent to the Divine and the limitless to the Necessity of the *Timaeus,* while the limit and the limited are the effect of the interworking of the two extremes. Pleasure belongs to the limitless, knowledge (of the sort embraced by science) to the limit. This return to the question of pleasure, now treated without the ascetic bias of the middle Dialogues, prepares us for the main ethical theme of the *Laws.*

The Laws

The life of man is discussed in relation to education, art, and religion, not measured by the Ideal criterion of happiness as in *The Republic,* but by practical considerations of pleasure. On this same basis a system of laws is devised, not for an ideal State, but for the best feasible State in which the individual may freely develop. This Dialogue is known to be the work of Plato's last days, and it is in many respects a summing up and revision of all his previous writings. Perhaps its most notable feature is the return to the religious convictions which were prominent in the earliest Dialogues.

The Minor Dialogues

These I have separated from the main groups, in some cases because they are trivial and probably spurious, and in other cases because, in essential matters, they do not advance upon one of the included Dialogues. In either case, it is well for the reader who approaches Plato for the first time to leave all of them, except perhaps the *Laches* and *Theages,* to the end. The *Menexenus,* in particular, raises the question of authenticity. Judging this Dialogue by intrinsic evidence alone, I should have been inclined to reject it as spurious, as some critics do not hesitate actually to do. Yet

Aristotle apparently accepted it as Platonic, and we know from Cicero that in his day it was so much admired as to be recited annually at Athens. Such testimony ought to instil modesty into the modern scholar. Some of the Dialogues, for example the *First* and *Second Alcibiades*, read as if they were composed by an accredited pupil of the Academy while Plato was still alive, and as such might be called semi-authentic. But this explanation, of course, I offer as pure conjecture.

The *Laches*, *Theages*, and *Lysis*, dealing respectively with courage, wisdom, and friendship, might form a class by themselves with the *Charmides*.

The *First* and *Second Alcibiades* have many points in common with the *Euthyphro*. The *Rivals* asks who the philosopher is, and answers that it is he who knows himself, and hence knows how to govern and give judgement. The *Hipparchus* debates the meaning of the profitable.

The *Hippias Major* is on the nature of beauty. The *Hippias Minor* discusses ignorance as the real source of evil. The *Io* deals with poetry and the poet, and the *Menexenus* with oratory.

The *Clitopho* shows Socrates taken to task because he has never given a positive definition of justice. It properly forms an introduction to *The Republic*. The *Critias*, an unfinished sequel to *The Republic* and *Timaeus*, was designed to narrate the heroic war of Athens with the mythical kingdom of Atlantis.

The *Minos*, on the nature of law, may be taken as introductory to the *Laws*. Its authenticity is doubtful. The *Epinomis*, which purports to be a continuation of the *Laws*, is in my judgement spurious.

To the body of the Dialogues is appended a collection

of thirteen *Letters,* which I have never been able to accept as genuine, despite their early admission into the canon by critics of antiquity. Whether genuine or not, they are an important source for the facts of Plato's life.

The brief *Definitions* of philosophic terms cannot be Plato's, but probably were composed for use in the Academy.

Finally, in some editions there are six Dialogues appended, all trivial, which are certainly spurious, and were so regarded in antiquity. They need not be considered.